Inspired by tradition. Kalevala poetry in Finnish music

INSPIRED BY TRADITION

Kalevala poetry in Finnish music

Inspired by tradition. Kalevala poetry in Finnish music

© Writers, translators and Finnish Music Information Centre Fimic, 2004

Editors: Jutta Jaakkola and Aarne Toivonen
Translation: Jaakko Mäntyjärvi,
Hanna-Mari Latham (Värttinä, p. 64–65) and
Laura Stark (The Kalevala's contents, p. 22–25)

Cover design: Jari Salo
Layout: Joonas Reijonen

Printed in Finland by Gummerus Kirjapaino Oy, Jyväskylä 2005

Finnish Music Information Centre Fimic
ISBN 952-5076-45-8

II Kalevala poetry in Finnish folk music

Timo Leisiö:
The runo code. The Finnish epic folk song tradition in Finland

Timo Leisiö & Helena Ruhkala:
The kantele. From the jaw of a pike to electric amplification

Pekko Käppi:
Ancient voices in the firmament of new folk music

III Kalevala poetry in Finnish classical music

Antti Häyrynen:
Kalevala poetry in Finnish classical music 66

IV Kalevala poetry in Finnish jazz

Petri Silas:
Kalevala poetry in Finnish jazz

> Karelia and Piirpauke blaze the trail (116) – Large-scale works (118) – Kukko and Vesala:
> multiculturalism and deeper shamanism (119) – Sarmanto and Pohjola: symphonic works and
> a strong Finnish flavour (121) – End of the millennium: a new generation (122) –
> Select discography & Further reading (123)

V Kalevala poetry in Finnish popular music

Hannu Tolvanen:
On the Kalevala tradition in Finnish popular music before the 1970s

> Kalevala elements in Finnish popular music (124) – The emergence of popular music:
> the music of cities and a new breed of tradition (125) – Proliferation of musical life (126) –
> The 'coupleteers' (127) – Noisy jazz, mambo and translated schlagers (128) –
> Why not until the 1970s? (128) – Further reading (129)

Petri Silas: The Kalevala and prog rock

Samuli Knuuti: "It's the language, you see."
The importance of the Kalevala in contemporary Finnish rock

> Unique relationship of rock lyrics to literature (132) – Runo singing in rock: the demand
> for good lyrics (133) – Ismo Alanko, heir to the shamans (134) – CMX and primeval
> alliteration (136) – Mythic ruggedness amidst sky channels (138) – Select discography &
> Further reading (138)

Matti Riekki: From the smithy of Ilmarinen.
Kalevala and heavy metal

Amorphis: The marriage of Kalevala and metal (139) – The legacy of Amorphis (140)
– Select discography & Further reading (143)

Foreword

This book is the first ever to explore the relationship of ancient Finnish *Kalevala* poetry and Finnish music in all genres of music. Plenty has been written about the Kalevala tradition in Finnish classical music, but here jazz and various forms of popular music are addressed too.

The poetry referenced here must be understood to include the entire ancient Finnish tradition and not just the *Kalevala* epic compiled by **Elias Lönnrot**. The tradition has also yielded for example the companion volume of lyrical poetry entitled the *Kanteletar* (1840) and the huge 34-volume compendium of collected folk poetry entitled *Suomen Kansan Vanhoja Runoja* (Ancient Poems of the Finnish People, 1908–1997), a unique and rich resource. All this material is governed by a single code of poetry unique in the world in its comprehensiveness that for thousands of years functioned as a single uniform system of expression for all life situations. As far as we know, no other culture has such a wide-ranging single code of poetry.

We will be celebrating the 170th anniversary of the first version of the *Kalevala* in 2005. The title of this book points in two directions in time: towards the ancient, rich tradition on one hand and towards the new, adventurous innovations inspired by it on the other.

Helsinki, September 5, 2004

Jutta Jaakkola and Aarne Toivonen
Finnish Music Information Centre

A LITHOGRAPH BY G. BUDKOWSKI FROM 1845, DEPICTING **Elias Lönnrot** AT THE TIME OF COMPILING THE SECOND VERSION OF THE *Kalevala*. PHOTO: FINNISH LITERATURE SOCIETY.

I

Introduction to Kalevala poetry

Pekka Laaksonen:

FROM ORAL TRADITION TO NATIONAL EPIC: ABOUT THE POETRY, THE COLLECTING AND ELIAS LÖNNROT'S KALEVALA

1 The Kalevala, Finland's national epic

The Kalevala was published in three different versions in 1835 (the first version), 1849 (the 'New Kalevala') and 1862 (an edition for schools). The middle one of these, the most extensive compilation comprising 50 *runos* or cantos totalling 22,795 lines, is the canonized version known today. The epic was compiled by **Elias Lönnrot** (1802–1884), partly inspired by the Enlightenment in central Europe and by the Romantic movement. Lönnrot's structural ideal was the Iliad of Homer.

With the *Kalevala*, the young nation took two enormous steps. It believed that it had discovered in its ancient poetry evidence of a glorious past, and the epic was thus a major boost to national self-esteem. But the national epic also brought Finland into the continuum of European civilization, raising the Finns to the rank of a historical people alongside the other historical peoples of Europe.

The *Kalevala* was not commissioned. However, Lönnrot and his epic could hardly have appeared on the scene in Finnish society much earlier nor indeed much later than they did. Earlier, the political and cultural framework would not have been in place; later, the cultural and historical impact of the epic would in any case have been less than it actually was. At just the right time, Lönnrot demonstrated with his work what a national cultural treasure was lurking in the oral tradition among the uneducated masses and how this tradition could be harnessed and made the foundation of the self-esteem and civilization of a young nation.

2 About the features of Finnish folk poetry

The Kalevala metre, a unique cultural code

One of the most important features of the *Kalevala* and of ancient Finnish poetry in general is its metre. The '*Kalevala* metre' is trochaic tetrameter, with a certain degree of freedom in the first foot of each line, which may have three or even four syllables instead of two (compare the standard *Vaka / vanha / Väinä- / möinen* with *Vaka oli / vanha / Väinä- / möinen*). A line never ends on a single-syllable word. Originally, this poetry was sung; indeed, the very word runo ('poem') originally meant 'singer'. The commonly recognized features of '*Kalevala style*' singing are narrow melodic compass, monophony and variation — the latter a typical feature of the poetry too. As the singing was non-stanzaic and narrow in compass, even the minutest variations took on great significance: this, indeed, was the huge richness of the musical world of this ancient tradition.

The emergence of *Kalevala* metre is an important indicator in tracing the history of our ancient folk poetry. The presence of this same metre in different languages is as sure a piece of evidence of a shared cultural heritage as archaeological finds or linguistic features. The *Kalevala* metre was known to the Finns, the Karelians, the Ingrians, the Votians (Ishorians) and the Estonians. In many areas, the ancient epic and lyrical poetry and spells were eventually crowded out by the newer rhymed poetry, but the metre persisted in proverbs and riddles.

The *Kalevala* metre was a very special code that functioned as a mnemonic aid for important things, preserving them in the collective memory of song. What was extraordinary about the metre was the scope of its application. It was used for epic poetry, lyrical poetry, spells, proverbs and riddles, and it was also the metre of rituals: bear wakes, weddings and seasonal festivals. Probably in no other culture has a single poetic metre held such a wide significance. This, of course, helped Lönnrot enormously: most of the material he collected, whatever its original context and age, was in the same metre and as such usable in the Kalevala.

The Kalevala and the genres of the Finnish folk poetry tradition

Kalevala poetry is not the only poetic genre in the Finnish folk tradition. Formally, Finnish folk poetry can be divided into two groups: *Kalevala* metre poetry and rhymed folk poetry. The *Kalevala* metre is supposed to have emerged during the Proto-Finnic period (2000 to 500 BC), at which point the language groups of the Baltic-Finnic branch had not yet fully diverged.

Kalevala metre poetry can in turn be divided on the basis of its content and context into epic poems, lyrical poems, spells and situational poems. Examples of the latter are laments, wedding poems, work songs and spells.

Rhymed folk songs began to appear in Finland in the 17th century with the decline of *Kalevala*-metre folk singing in western Finland. By the 19th century, the brief rhymed stanzaic songs known as rekilaulu (literally 'sleigh song', though possibly a corruption of the German *Reigenlied*) had spread throughout the land. Alongside the folk poetry there is a rich oral tradition of prose featuring tales, stories, myths of origin, legends and numerous sub-genres and variants of these.

3 Finnish folk poetry collecting before Lönnrot

From the Reformation to the Enlightenment

In compiling the *Kalevala*, Elias Lönnrot by no means had to start from scratch. Finnish folk poetry collecting had been going on for quite some time before him, ever since the Reformation in the 16th century. **Mikael Agricola (1510–1557)**, who translated the Bible into Finnish and is credited with developing the written Finnish language almost single-handedly, was the first known collector and publisher of folk poetry. In the foreword to his translation of the *Psalms,* he lists a number of pagan deities worshiped by the Finns, which demonstrates that Agricola had an interest in the life and culture of the common people. Nevertheless, the purpose of that rhymed foreword was to expose superstitions and promote their eradication.

Systematic collecting of folk tradition began in Sweden-Finland in 1630 with a memorandum signed by King Gustavus II Adolphus concerning the collecting of ancient relics. The memorandum advised that attention should be paid to old heroic tales and spells, and even the tunes to which poems were sung. The Kingdom of Sweden was becoming a major power in the region around that time, and this memorandum represented an effort on the part of its leadership to reinforce the identity of the realm in the area of culture alongside politics.

In Sweden, this memorandum led to imaginative heroic historical chronicles of ancient times in Sweden. It was in this spirit that **Daniel Juslenius** (1676–1752) compared Finnish folk poetry with the pastoral poetry of Antiquity, and he spared no hyperbole in claiming of Finnish poetry that "its charm, power to move the soul and power to express cannot be exhaustively described in a few words; and even if I could, I might not convince anyone not familiar with the essence of that language".

De poesi Fennica by H.G. Porthan

Enlightenment scholar **Henrik Gabriel Porthan** (1739–1804) was a significant figure in the study of folk tradition. He saw the harsh realities of life and hard work that underlay folk poems, but on the other hand he also understood how important folk poetry was for the development of Finnish literature and culture.

Porthan published his findings on folk poetry in *De poesi Fennica.* Its first part was published in 1766–1768 and its highly interesting second part in 1778. The first part is a study of the structure of the poetry, mainly on the basis of the theory of poetics. In the second part, he focuses on peasant poets, the genres of folk poetry, the performance practices, the 'milling poems' performed by women and, in the final chapter, spells.

His planned sequel was never realized. It is interesting that Porthan was the first scholar to draw attention to the musical features of folk poetry: the foreword hints at Porthan having intended to print the melodies of *runo* songs using letters for pitches.

Porthan grasped the concept of comparative study of poetry, but even more importantly he believed that the fragments and versions he had uncovered might yield a coherent narrative — an idea without which Lönnrot would probably never have dared embark on the task of compiling the *Kalevala*.

K.A. Gottlund pitches the idea of a Finnish epic

Karl Axel Gottlund (1796–1875) was fascinated by folk poetry not so much because of its imaginativeness or beauty as because of its pedagogical nature and common-sense wisdom. He surmised that the Finns had earlier been a civilized people but had then degenerated into Medieval barbarism. He felt that the ancient poems demonstrated that the Finns had a noble prehistory, an age of heroes, in their past.

Gottlund had a grand romantic dream: perhaps it would be possible to construct an extensive narrative on the basis of the ancient poems. He wrote his now famous quote: "If we should collect the ancient folk songs and organize them into a methodical whole, whether it be an epic, a drama or any other thing, it might become a new Homer, *Ossian* or *Nibelungenlied*."

We cannot conclusively prove that these particular words were what Lönnrot took to heart. But this, in any case, in the first documented instance of the idea of an epic based on Finnish folk poetry.

4 Elias Lönnrot and the birth of the Kalevala

Lönnrot enrolled at the University in Turku in October 1822, simultaneously with two other future leaders of Finnish literature and nationalism, **Johan Ludvig Runeberg** (1804–1877) and **Johan Vilhelm Snellman** (1806–1881). Lönnrot, the shy but gifted son of a tailor in Sammatti, was the only one of the three who spoke Finnish as his mother tongue.

Lönnrot on Väinämöinen's trail

Lönnrot's most important teacher at university was **Reinhold von Becker** (1788–1858) who had himself gone on an expedition to northern Finland to collect Finnish folk poetry. On the basis of the fairly extensive material he had gathered, von Becker wrote an article on Väinämöinen. Contrary to the then received conception, he saw Väinämöinen as a multi-skilled person and a great warrior that only the simple could regard as a demigod.

von Becker gave Lönnrot his unfinished articles, his considerable body of collected poetry and his mythological notes to study. The outcome of this was Lönnrot's dissertation, *De Wäinämöine, priscorum fennorum numine* (On Väinämöinen, god of the ancient Finns). Only a fragment of the dissertation has survived, but its importance was in that Lönnrot had now become acquainted with the largest collection of folk poetry assembled until then.

The wanderer goes off in search of poetry

In spring 1828, Lönnrot decided to embark on his first collecting expedition. His goal was to travel as far as the Government of Arkhangelsk, where the area of Vuokkiniemi had proved particularly rich in the ancient tradition. He never got to Russian Karelia on this expedition, however. The high point of the trip was meeting **Juhana Kainulainen** (1788–1847) in Kesälahti, who sang to him a long tale of Lemminkäinen, the tale of the singing competition between

Väinämöinen and Joukahainen, a fragment of the stealing of the Sampo and several long spells, 49 poems in all.

After the trip, Lönnrot began to edit the poetry for printing: the eventually five-part collection entitled *Kantele* — its full title was *Kantele taikka Suomen Kansan sekä Wanhoja että Nykysempiä Runoja ja Lauluja* (Kantele, or old and newer poems and songs of the Finnish people) — was published between 1829 and 1831. It contained 90 old poems and 20 newer ones. Lönnrot continued his expeditions, the third of which, in summer 1932, finally took him briefly to Viena Karelia.

Prelude to the Kalevala while working as a district physician in Kainuu

After completing his studies in Turku, Lönnrot went on to study medicine in Helsinki, and in January 1833 he moved to Kajaani to take up the post of district physician. Kajaani was not far from the lands of folk poetry, and indeed the town was the first stop for itinerant peddlers coming from Karelia. Lönnrot had become interested in drawing up portraits in poetry of the main heroes of the ancient poems: Väinämöinen, Lemminkäinen and Ilmarinen. It was with the tale of Väinämöinen in mind that Lönnrot went on his second trip to Russian Karelia.

In Vuonninen, he met the remarkable **Ontrei Malinen** (1781–1856), who sang to him nine extensive poems about Väinämöinen. However, Lönnrot's encounter with the old wise man **Vaassila Kieleväinen** (c. 1755–c. 1840) that same evening proved to be even more important. Vaassila's memory was failing, and he could only remember extracts from the major poems, but he was able to recite the narrative order of the poems when prompted. This was when Lönnrot began to conceive a single entity containing all the main heroic poems of the tradition. Indeed, some point to Lönnrot's evening with Vaassila as the moment when the notion of the *Kalevala* was born.

Vaassila, Arhippa Perttunen and the first version of the Kalevala, 1835

Having returned home, Lönnrot drew up a narrative poem about Väinämöinen as he had planned, but he was now increasingly caught up in his ambition to produce an entire epic. He found reassurance in Homer, since Karelian folk poems could surely be combined into a narrative worthy of the ancient Greeks — after all, they closely resembled the heroic poetry of the Greek oral tradition.

In winter 1834, he fashioned 16 songs or runos consisting of slightly over 5,000 lines. This was *Runokokous Väinämöisestä* (Poetry Collection on Väinämöinen), also known as the 'Ur-Kalevala'. However, by then Lönnrot had already decided to continue collecting poetry until he had enough material for a work corresponding to at least half of what Homer had done.

Lönnrot thus set out on his fifth expedition with the aim of collecting poems as long and as complete as possible from famous singers. He met **Arhippa Perttunen** (c. 1750–1841), the greatest of all *runo* singers, in the village of Latvajärvi in April 1834. Over more than two days, Perttunen sang to him long and complete poems in perfectly coherent order, totalling over 4,000 lines. This was beyond Lönnrot's wildest dreams. He now had enough material to expand his sketch, completed in the previous autumn, into a grand poetic work. His material totalled over 700 versions of poems, nearly 28,000 lines of field notes. The majority of these he had written down himself. On February 28, 1835, Lönnrot completed his labour, which he now entitled *Kalevala taikka Vanhoja Karjalan Runoja Suomen kansan muinosista ajoista* (Kalevala, or old Karelian poems about the ancient history of the Finnish people). February 28 is still celebrated in Finland as Kalevala Day and the Day of Finnish Culture.

The Kalevala as a depiction of Finland's ancient history

Lönnrot was certain that the heroes of the poems were historical persons. Based on the poems, he had reconstructed an ancient Kalevala age and its events. This also drew on the then current notions of the Asian origins of the Finno-Ugric peoples, but also on the Old Testament description of Israel's trek through the wilderness to the Promised Land. The Karelians, Tavastians and Estonians had also, the thinking went, left their Asian home under the leadership of their elder, Kaleva, and having crossed the Ural Mountains had arrived on the banks of the Volga and so onward to their present lands.

Lönnrot placed the events of the ancient poems on the southern shores of the White Sea in pagan times. Lönnrot cut all Christian and other later elements from the *Kalevala*, believing that he had thus returned the poems to their original guise. He assumed that the poems had originally emerged in the same order as the events described in them. He understood that the content of the poems had been better preserved than their form.

The Kalevala goes abroad

Immediately after its publication, the *Kalevala* was hailed as an ancient epic from pagan times. Lönnrot was understood only to have assembled the poems in the correct order. Parallels were drawn between the *Kalevala* and Homer, the *Edda* and the *Nibelungenlied*. This, of course, was of huge importance to the Finnish nation, which was only just finding its way in the world and seeking a meaningful history. However, this was a misconception that, once established, led folk poetry scholarship seriously astray for a long time.

The first version of the *Kalevala* was soon translated into Swedish, and in 1845, German fairy-tale and mythology scholar **Jacob Grimm** (1786–1863) gave a notable lecture on the epic of the Finns at the Science Academy in Berlin. He put the origin of the *Kalevala* even further back than the supposed heroic pagan era, to the ancient mists of mythology. Thus, the interest of foreign scholars in Finnish folk poetry, and their respect for it, had been awakened.

The travels of Daniel Europaeus and the 'New Kalevala'

The first version of the *Kalevala* was printed in an edition of 500 copies, which lasted over ten years. It was not, one might say, a hot seller. Once the edition had finally been sold out and a new edition was being planned, poetry collectors were charged with the task of finding the poems still missing from the Kalevala or of completing poems already known. New villages where the oral tradition survived were sought out, and new singers encountered, but collectors also returned to the singers who were already well known.

The most important of the new generation of collectors was **Daniel Europaeus** (1820–1884). In July 1845, he had several villagers sing to him in Mekrijärvi in Ilomantsi, the single most important village for folk poetry in Finland; the most important singers, however, were **Simana Sissonen** (1786–1846) and **Simana Huohvanainen** (1771–1858), who were conversant with the epic poetry of the *Kalevala* tradition. It has been estimated that Sissonen knew even more poems than Arhippa Perttunen. Europaeus collected much more poetry than Lönnrot, but then he also travelled more. It was not for nothing that it was said that Europaeus travelled "between the White Sea and Lake Ladoga like between two villages".

Into the canon of world literature: the 'New Kalevala' 1849

Lönnrot was convinced that all the poems of the *Kalevala* had been discovered. However, he no longer believed as he had in compiling the first version of the *Kalevala* that the old poems could be restored to their original form, even in terms of content. He also recognized that he knew more about folk poetry than any of the *runo* singers could ever know. All this made him much bolder in editing his material. Lönnrot remarked in a letter that, from the material he then had, he would have been able to put together seven *Kalevalas*, all different.

Lönnrot signed the preface to the 'New Kalevala' on April 17, 1849. The *Kalevala* is recognized as one of the great epics of world literature and, translated into 60 languages, it has aroused interest all over the world. It has been a direct source of inspiration for later poems, including the Estonian *Kalevipoeg*, **Henry Wadsworth Longfellow's** (1807–1882) *Song of Hiawatha* and parts of **J.R.R. Tolkien's** (1892–1973) *Lord of the Rings*. No other Finnish work of literature has become so well-known outside the country as the *Kalevala*, and no other Finnish work has had so diverse and profound an influence on national and international culture.

Further reading

Anneli Asplund and **Sirkka-Liisa Mettomäki**: *Kalevala* (www.finlit.fi/kalevala) - This excellent page at the Suomalaisen Kirjallisuuden Seura (Finnish Literature Society) site contains a short introduction to the *Kalevala* in Dutch, English, Estonian, Finnish, French, German, Polish, Portuguese, Spanish and Swedish, including the complete *Kalevala* text in Finnish.

⋮ Elias Lönnrot's first *Kalevala* (1835) was released in a first edition of 500
⋮ copies, which took over ten years to sell. Photo: Finnish Literature Society.

Anneli Asplund & Sirkka-Liisa Mettomäki:
The Kalevala's contents

Poems 1–2 ~ Ilmatar (the Virgin of the Air) descends to the waters. A pochard lays its eggs on her knee. The eggs break and the world is formed from their pieces. The mother of the water then gives birth to Väinämöinen. Sampsa Pellervoinen sows the forest trees. One of the trees, an oak, grows so large that it blots out both the sun and the moon. A tiny man rises from the sea and fells the giant oak. The sun and moon can shine once again.

Poems 3–4 ~ Joukahainen challenges Väinämöinen to a contest of wisdom and is defeated. With his singing, Väinämöinen causes Joukahainen to sink into a swamp. In order to save himself, Joukahainen promises his sister's hand in marriage to Väinämöinen. Upon learning of the bargain, the sister Aino mourns her fate and finally drowns herself.

Poems 5–7 ~ Väinämöinen searches the sea for Aino and catches her (she has been transformed into a fish) on his fishing hook. However, he loses her again and sets out to woo the maiden of Pohjola, the daughter of the North Farm. Meanwhile, eager for revenge, Joukahainen watches out for Väinämöinen on the way to Pohjola and shoots Väinämöinen's horse from underneath him as he rides across a river. Väinämöinen falls into the water and floats out to sea. There an eagle rescues him and carries him to Pohjola's shores. The mistress of Pohjola, Louhi, tends Väinämöinen until he recovers. In order to be able to return home, Väinämöinen promises that Ilmarinen the smith will forge a Sampo for Pohjola. The maiden of Pohjola, Louhi's daughter, is promised to the smith in return for the Sampo.

Poems 8–9 ~ On his way home, Väinämöinen meets the maiden of Pohjola and asks her to marry him. She agrees on the condition that Väinämöinen carry out certain impossible tasks. While Väinämöinen carves a wooden boat, his axe slips and he receives a deep wound in his knee. He searchers for an expert blood-stauncher and finally finds an old man who stops the flow of blood by using magic incantations.

Poem 10 ~ Using magic means, Väinämöinen sends the unwilling Ilmarinen to Pohjola. Ilmarinen forges the Sampo. Louhi shuts it inside a hill of rock. Ilmarinen is forced to return home without his promised bride.

Poems 11–12 ~ Lemminkäinen sets off to woo Kyllikki, a maiden of Saari Island. He makes merry with the other maidens and abducts Kyllikki. He later abandons her and leaves to woo the maiden of Pohjola. With his singing he bewitches the people of Pohjola to leave the farmhouse at North Farm. Only one person, a cowherd, does not fall under his spell.

Poems 13–15 ~ Lemminkäinen asks Louhi for her daughter, but Louhi demands that he first hunt and kill the Devil's elk, then the Devil's fire-breathing gelding, and finally the swan in Tuonela River, which is the boundary between this world and the next. There the vengeful cowherd kills Lemminkäinen and throws his body into the river. Lemminkäinen's mother receives a sign of her son's death and goes out in search of him. She rakes the pieces of her son's body out of Tuonela River, puts them back together and brings her son back to life.

Poems 16–17 ~ Väinämöinen begins to build a boat and visits Tuonela in order to ask for the magic spells need to finish it. He does not find them. He then seeks the missing spells from the stomach of the ancient wise man, Antero Vipunen, who has long been dead. He finds them and finishes his boat.

Poems 18–19 ~ Väinämöinen sets off in his boat to woo the daughter of Pohjola, but she chooses instead Ilmarinen, the forger of the Sampo. Ilmarinen successfully performs the three impossible tasks set before him: he plows a field full of vipers, hunts down the bear of Tuonela and the wolf of Manala and finally fishes the Great Pike out of the Tuonela River. Louhi promises her daughter to Ilmarinen.

Poems 20–25 ~ In Pohjola, preparations are made for the wedding and invitations are sent to all except Lemminkäinen. The groom and his folk arrive in Pohjola, and there is great feasting. Väinämöinen entertains the wedding guests with his singing. The bride and groom are given advice concerning marriage, and the bride bids farewell to her people and departs with Ilmarinen for Kalevala. There a banquet is also ready for the guests. Väinämöinen sings the praises of the wedding guests.

Poems 26–27 ~ Lemminkäinen shows up at the banquet in Pohjola uninvited, and demands food and drink. He is offered a tankard of beer filled with vipers. Lemminkäinen engages the master of Pohjola in a singing contest and a swordfight and kills him.

Poems 28–30 ~ Lemminkäinen flees the people of Pohjola who are rising up in arms against him and hides on Saari Island, living among the maidens of the island until he is forced to flee once again, this time from the island's jealous menfolk. Lemminkäinen finds his home in ashes and his mother hiding in a cottage in the forest. Lemminkäinen sets out to seek revenge on Pohjola, but is forced to return home because a cold spell cast by the mistress of Pohjola has frozen his ships in the sea.

Poems 31–34 ~ Brothers Untamo and Kalervo quarrel violently, Kalervo's troop is slain, and of his kin only his son Kullervo remains. Because of his superhuman powers, Kullervo fails in every task he is given. Untamo sells the boy to Ilmarinen as a serf. The wife of Ilmarinen send Kullervo out to be a cowherd and out of spite bakes a stone into the bread which is his only provisions. Kullervo breaks his knife on the stone while trying to cut the bread, and in revenge drives the cows into the swamp and brings home a pack of wild animals instead. The mistress, intending to milk the cows, is mauled to death. Kullervo flees. He finds his family in the forest, but hears that his sister has disappeared.

Poems 35–36 ~ Kullervo's father sends him to pay the taxes. On his return trip, Kullervo unwittingly seduces his sister, who then drowns herself in the rapids upon discovering the truth. Kullervo sets out to seek revenge from Untamo. Having killed Untamo and his family, Kullervo returns home to find is own family dead. Kullervo commits suicide.

Poem 37 ~ Ilmarinen mourns the death of his wife and decides to forge a woman of gold. The golden maiden remains, however, lifeless and cold. Väinämöinen warns the young people against worshipping gold.

Poem 38 ~ Ilmarinen is rejected by the youngest daughter of Pohjola and carries her off in his sleigh. The girl reviles Ilmarinen and so offends him that he finally turns her into a seagull with his singing. Ilmarinen tells Väinämöinen of the wealth and prosperity that the Sampo has brought the people of Pohjola.

Poems 39–41 ~ Väinämöinen, Ilmarinen and Lemminkäinen set out to steal the Sampo from Pohjola. In the course of the journey, their boat runs aground on the shoulders of a giant pike. Väinämöinen kills the pike and fashions a kantele from its jawbone. No one else is able to play the instrument, but Väinämöinen holds all living things spellbound with his playing.

Poems 42–43 ~ Väinämöinen puts the people of Pohjola to sleep with his kantele playing and the Sampo is taken to the travellers' boat and rowed away. The people of Pohjola awaken and Louhi, the mistress of Pohjola, sends obstacles in the path of the raiders to hinder their escape. The seafarers survive, but the kantele falls into the sea. Louhi sets off in pursuit and transforms herself into a giant bird of prey. In the ensuing battle the Sampo is smashed and falls into the sea. Some of the fragments remain in the sea, but others wash ashore and bring Finland good fortune and prosperity. Louhi is left with only the worthless lid of the Sampo and an impoverished land.

Poem 44 ~ In vain, Väinämöinen seeks the kantele which fell into the sea. He makes a new kantele from birchwood and his playing once again delights the whole of creation.

Poem 45–46 ~ Louhi sends diseases to destroy the people of Kalevala, but Väinämöinen cures the sick. Louhi sends a bear to attack the Kalevala cattle, but Väinämöinen slays the bear. The people of Kalevala organize a bear-killing feast.

Poems 47–48 ~ The mistress of Pohjola hides the sun and the moon inside a hill and steals the fire as well. Ukko, the supreme god, makes a new sun and moon by striking fire, but the fire falls to earth, into the belly of a giant fish. Väinämöinen asks Ilmarinen to go fishing with him. They catch the fish and place the fire in the service of humankind.

Poem 49 ~ Ilmarinen forges a new sun and moon, but they do not shine. After battling the people of Pohjola, Väinämöinen returns to ask Ilmarinen to fashion a set of keys with which to release the sun and moon from Pohjola's mountain. While Ilmarinen is forging, Louhi sets the sun and moon free to return to their places in the sky.

Poem 50 ~ Marjatta conceives a child from a whortleberry. Her baby boy is born in the forest, but soon disappears, to be found finally in a swamp. Väinämöinen condemns the fatherless child to death, but the child speaks out against the sentence and is christened King of Karelia. Väinämöinen departs in a copper boat with the prediction that he will be needed again someday to make a new Sampo for the people, to bring new light and play new songs.

Translated by Laura Stark
(Source: www.finlit.fi/kalevala)

Characters and concepts in the Kalevala

This list only covers a fraction of the names of characters, places and concepts in the *Kalevala*. The ones selected here are those that come up the most frequently in the context of music.

Aino is a character derived from a poem from Dvina Karelia about a maiden who hangs herself. Lönnrot changed her fundamentally: in the *Kalevala*, she is a young woman who drowns herself rather than agree to marry old man Väinämöinen. Aino reappears later as a strange fishlike creature that Väinämöinen tries in vain to catch.

Ilmarinen or Ilmari, a smith, appears in over half of all the poems in the *Kalevala*. His principal achievements are the taming of iron, the forging of the Sampo, the wooing of the Maiden of Pohjola and the release of the captive lights of heaven from Pohjola. Ilmarinen's CV also includes forging the vault of heaven. Lönnrot highlighted the importance of Ilmarinen at many junctures.

Kaleva, Kalevala. One of the overall dramaturgical structures of Lönnrot's epic is the tension between the peoples of Kaleva (the good guys) and Pohja (the bad guys). The personal name Kaleva has sometimes been identified with the ancient giant Kaleva, whose offspring are supposed to include Väinämöinen, Ilmarinen and Lemminkäinen. The name itself possibly comes from the Lithuanian word *kálvis* ('blacksmith'); the smith-god Kalevias is an important hero in ancient Baltic and Proto-Finnic lore too. Kalevala is a concept invented by Lönnrot to refer to the homeland of the people of Kaleva.

Kullervo, son of Kalervo, is the protagonist in Runos 31 to 36, a tale of 2,196 lines that is considered Lönnrot's finest achievement. The tale of this tragic hero is told almost like a classical tragedy, although the original elements appear in very different guises in different regions. The main features of the tale include: working as a herdsman for Ilmarinen's wife, breaking his knife on a stone and raising the predators of the forest to tear Ilmarinen's wife apart; finding his family, who he believed to have been killed; unwittingly seducing his own sister; and finally throwing himself on his sword.

Kyllikki (Runo 11) is a beautiful maiden whom Lemminkäinen abducts from the island of Saari. They make a pact whereby Lemminkäinen will not go to war if Kyllikki does not go out wandering in the village. After Kyllikki breaks her side of the pact, Lemminkäinen dons his armour. The original folk poetry paints Kyllikki as a stronger and more mature woman than the one we see in the *Kalevala*. She was originally a powerful character, quite the equal of the male heroes.

Lemminkäinen is a quicksilvery Don Juan character who appears in four episodes: he abducts and then abandons Kyllikki (Runos 11 and 12); he undertakes a number of exploits including hunting the Devil's elk to win the hand of the Maiden of Pohjola

(Runos 12 to 14) but falls into the River of Tuonela, the land of the dead, whence his mother rescues him (Runos 14 and 15); he then kills the Master of Pohjola (Runos 26 and 27) and takes refuge with the maidens of Saari only to go on yet another expedition to Pohjola (Runos 28 to 30); and, finally, he participates in the Sampo expedition (Runos 39 to 43). (See also p. 71)

Luonnotar (literally 'nature-daughter') is one of several rather vaguely defined female beings. In Runo 1 of the *Kalevala*, Lönnrot mentions that Luonnotar gave birth to Väinämöinen. The duty of a *luonnotar* is usually to warn against future perils, much like the Norns in Old Norse mythology or the Fates in Greek mythology.

Pohjola, Pohja is the homeland of the enemies of the people of Kaleva. It is the place where the Sampo is forged and whence it is eventually stolen to be brought to Kaleva. Pohjola is described as a cold and dark place from which travellers rarely return. Pohjola is associated sometimes with Lapland and sometimes with Tuonela, the Underworld of the *Kalevala*.

Sampo is a concept comparable in its enigmatic nature to the myth of Atlantis and its various explanations. The tradition of explanations of the Sampo goes back to 1818, and they can be divided into the cosmological, the concrete-historical and the abstract. In the folk poetry tradition, it is never explicitly stated what exactly the Sampo is, except that it is an object which is forged out of metal and which generates happiness and richness. The Sampo is also associated with the people of Pohjola. Previously, the Sampo has been variously explained as a mill, the sun, a shaman drum, a dragon ship or the world pole around which the firmament revolves. Cognate words have been sought in Slovene, Mongolian and Tibetan, and in the 20th century the Sampo has been given such meanings as a symbol of astral sacrality or a cult phenomenon, and with the aid of astronomy it can be seen as a combination of a phallus and a millstone constituting a fertility symbol. The enigma appears impenetrable, new theories notwithstanding.

Tapio and Tapiola. Tapio is the king of the forest, and Tapiola is the abode of his people. He was the god to pray to when going out to hunt and when requesting safety for cattle grazing in the forest. In one version of the tale of Väinämöinen's Orphic music-making that attracted the denizens of water and forest, Tapio was present too.

Tuoni or Tuonela is the Underworld of the *Kalevala*. The most important of the Tuonela tales is Runo 14, where Lemminkäinen shoots the Swan of Tuonela. Runo 16 is also important, with Väinämöinen going to Tuonela to seek the words of power that he lacks. The journey is an obviously shamanist one: he returns from the trip in the shape of a snake, an image well in tune with the conceptions that Arctic peoples have of shamans going into a trance. The cartography of the *Kalevala* also includes the River of Tuonela, a counterpart of the Greek River Styx.

Väinämöinen or **Väinö** is one of the most important characters in the *Kalevala*, appearing in Runos 1–10, 16–21, 25 and 35–50. Väinämöinen was not the main character in the poetry of the tradition in all regions; in Estonia, for instance, he is unknown. Despite this, Lönnrot turned the old wizard into the central protagonist, played down his mythological properties and highlighted his human and historical features. Väinämöinen has been interpreted in a number of ways in different times and by different writers: he has variously been described as a 'forger of songs' and a hero-poet, a son of the ancient giant Kaleva and the Apollo-Orpheus of Finland. In the original folk poetry, Väinämöinen is in turn a creator-god, a cultural hero, a shaman, a suitor or a naval hero. Väinämöinen embodies the creative power of the *Kalevala* and of the Finnish people: he is a person capable of filling the roles of light-bringer, educator, war hero and leader of the people.

Pekka Laaksonen: The *Kanteletar*

Of all collections of Finnish folk poetry, the *Kanteletar* (1840) has been a particular favourite among Finnish composers of vocal music. This collection of lyrical and lyrical-epic poems was the middle one of Lönnrot's three great publications, coming between the first and second editions of the *Kalevala* in 1840. Lönnrot went on to conclude his career with a collection of spells published in his old age (1880).

After the publication of the first *Kalevala* in 1835, Lönnrot took up the recording and compiling of the lyrical poems he had collected during his travels. The first sketches of the *Kanteletar* were completed in 1838, and Lönnrot further expanded the collection in the same year. This collection, whose full title is *Kanteletar taikka Suomen kansan vanhoja lauluja ja virsiä* (Kanteletar, or old songs and hymns of the Finnish people), mostly contains material collected by Lönnrot himself, although it incorporates some folk poems published earlier.

The *Kanteletar* comprises 652 poems and over 22,000 lines, twice as much material as the first *Kalevala*. The first part of the *Kanteletar* contains lyrical songs, which Lönnrot grouped into songs for general occasions, wedding songs, herding songs and children's songs. The second part is divided into songs of girls, women, boys and men according to their assumed performers. The third part is a collection of historical poems, romances, legends, ballads and other lyrical-epic poems.

The material for the *Kanteletar* came mostly from Finnish Karelia, with very little material from east of the border. Lönnrot singles out two sources for mention, **Mateli Kuivalatar** (1771–1846) of Ilomantsi and **Juhana Kainulainen** (1788–1847) of Kesälahti.

Compiling the *Kanteletar* before publishing the final version of the *Kalevala* is significant in two ways. Firstly, in the lyrical poetry of the *Kanteletar* Lönnrot was freed of his dependence on the source material and was able to edit the poetry according to the aesthetic principles he had adopted earlier. On the other hand, the *Kanteletar* also served as a source for the 'New Kalevala' (1849): at least 2,000 lines found their way from the *Kanteletar* into the national epic, most significantly the Kullervo stories and certain lyrical interludes.

The *Kanteletar* has had an enormous impact on Finnish literature and art. Being a collection of short, lyrical poems, it has also lent itself excellently to musical settings. The world of the *Kanteletar* may be encountered in the choral music of Sibelius and contemporary jazz alike.

Timo Leisiö:

STYLISTIC ELEMENTS OF RUNO SONG

It is important to note that the published and printed *Kalevala* is a textual unit, an epic for readers. However, the origin of the *runos* of the *Kalevala* is in an oral tradition: the *Kalevala* was composed of various Baltic-Finnic song-poems once used for ritual and magical purposes and for entertainment. Myths and charms were performed by singing because singing was the most effective code to communicate with powers and beings of the Otherworld. The Finns knew these songs as *runo* or *virsi* or *laulu*, each word ultimately going back to the idea of a magical charm and mythical knowledge. Some poetic themes go back to the Mesolithic, while others were composed in the 18th and 19th centuries.

1 Basic concepts of runo music

Syllabic treatment of text

During and before the Bronze Age (c. 1900–500 BC), there were no fixed metric patterns. The length of a melodic line could vary substantially. However, it appears that even in those day people preferred to sing one tone to one syllable. The emergence of the *Kalevala* metre stemmed from an elementary innovation which occurred in northern Estonia and south-western Finland late in the second millennium BC: the metric pattern of the poetic line consolidated into four stressed and four unstressed positions. Each position had an equal duration, and singers only put one syllable in each position. As an exception to this, the first two positions could hold two syllables each. The *runo* line is thus octosyllabic, though it may exceptionally contain nine or ten syllables instead of eight. There are no metrically empty positions in *Kalevala* metre and thus no upbeat.

Iterative form

A *runo* song was iterative by form. Before the 17th century, strophic structures did not exist. Ideally, singing was a repetition either of one melodic line *(a a a)* or of two melodic lines *(ab ab ab)*. In some cases, a two-line unit closely resembles the yoik of the northern Sámi in that the latter line may differ from the former only by a tone or two. In other respects, however, the stylistic grammars of *yoik* and *runo* are very different.

Runo songs often had only three, four or five tones, but because of their modal complexity they yielded a great richness to their listeners.

Transposing series of natural tones

What has escaped music scholars is the human capacity to transpose a modal structure of tones from one pitch to another. This occurs unconsciously and is a species-specific ability of all humans. There are *runo* tunes which have a very rudimentary idea of transposing a series of natural tones from one position to another. The melodies are not composed of one mode; they are composed of two clusters of pitches picked up from the simplest natural tones. For instance, these pitches in the series with C as its fundamental are numbers 4–5–6–7–8 *(c–e–g–bb–c)*. If transposed up a fifth to G, the same numbers correspond to the pitches *g–b–d–f–g*. The singers simply chose one, two or three tones from both clusters and improvised long poems swinging between the clusters with the pitches C and G as their fundamentals. (A western listener interprets this as a simple tonal tune on C and G major chords, which is an anachronistic failure.) The following tune is based on this technique. (The two series of natural pitches in C and G are given below the melody, and the numerical symbols of these pitches are shown as numbers above the staff.)

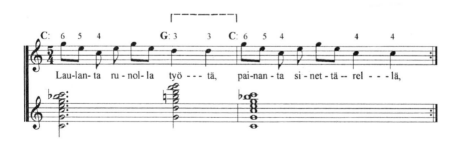

In the *runo* tradition there are melodies that are genetically — i.e. on the level of musical grammar — related to the Sámi *yoik* or Native American music or Australian aboriginal songs. These archaic musics are only *seemingly* tonal, but explaining this further is beyond the scope of the present introduction.

Melodies based on modal incipits

Terms like 'tonal' and 'pentatonic' are well known. However, they are not valid as analytical concepts when dealing with traditions beyond western tonality or the pentatonic system found in Mongolia, China, the Andes, and so on. There is a huge collection of melodic traditions in the world that must be described as *pre-hexatonal* and *prepentatonal* (with the prefix to -*tonal* referring to the number of intervals in an octave). The latter *(prepentatonal)* means that the tunes are not based on pentatonic grammar but on the modal *incipits* (i.e. rudimentary formations) of pentatonic modes. These incipits may seem quite vague. The Finnish song *Nuku nuku nurmilintu* (Sleep, sleep, little bird) is a spell used as a lullaby; it is based on the prepentatonal incipit *SOL on g^1 *(sol–la—do–re–mi)*.

Prehexatonal incipits were germs for six hexatonal roots, three of which went on to evolve into the roots of the western modes of major, natural minor and harmonic minor. The lyrical song *Oravainen* about a squirrel is based on the hexatonal root *g*–IV with its fundamental tone $5 = g^1$ as the apex of the melody. In any hexatonal mode, the main elements are that its fundamental pitch corresponds to the dominant in tonal theory and that the tonal sixth degree is missing.

A *runo* tune is seldom based on one mode. Instead, a singer might modulate from one mode to another as soon as (s)he changed the position of the fundamental or transposed a mode a second or a third or a fourth downwards and returned back again. Sometimes these melodies are quite simple, but in many cases there is a complicated and quite non-tonal idea underlying the melody. In the tune *Tuo oli vanha Väinämöinen* (Old man Väinämöinen), the melody opens in incipit *II with g^1 as its fundamental pitch $(g^1-b^1-c^2\#-d^2-e^2-f^2)$. In the second measure, it modulates to *f*-based root IV, the mother mode of natural minor. This tune is both strange and familiar to a modern listener, and for a simple reason: it is not tonal but pre-tonal.

Noin sanoi emo tytölle (Mother advised her daughter) represents another solution. First, the singer uses the incipit *IV on g, transposing it from the fundamental g^1 up to c^2 and back. In the last measure, there is a drastic modulation to the incipit *f-*VI $(f^1-a^1-c^2)$. However, starting the next line is easy because the final tone c^2 also is the 3rd degree of *g*–*IV (corresponding to the tonic of C minor).

The essence of runo modalities

The most typical feature of archaic *runo* melodies is fusing hemitonic hexatonal modes with unhemitonic prepentatonal modes, resulting in various kinds of fusion modality. (In other words: the essence of *runo* tunes is that they are simultaneously diatonic and pentatonic.) An independent fusion modality like this is called *mictic*, which term is derived from a Greek term meaning 'blended, mixed, intermingled'. There are various mictic regions in Europe (such as Irish and Scottish) but the *runo* differs from the rest of Europe in its micticism. In runo tunes, the amalgamated elements are prepentatonal and (pre)hexatonal — but this is a trait that sometimes governs Finnish folk music beyond the *runo* tradition even today. Mictic melodies are archaic and typical of, say, the northern Sámi *yoik*, Ainu singing in Japan and Native American singing.

The mictic modes are usually modulated or transposed, and consequently there are few melodies based on a single unchanging mictos. The pastoral song *Muut ne pannah paimenie* (Other people employ the cowherds) represents a single mictos: it is pointless to guess whether it is prepentatonic (LA mode on c^2) or based on the incipit of C minor mode. It is both. This also is the case in *Ite vanha Väinämöinen* (It was old man Väinämöinen), which is a mictic fusion of modes DO on c^2 and g–I (> C Major)

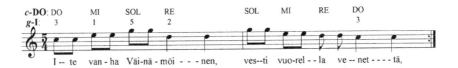

2 About rhythm

The rhythm of runic songs is a metre of eight positions called *morae*. Singing was mainly syllabic. Where one poetic line corresponded to one melodic line, the metre of the music was either 2/4 or 5/4 (2+3/4 or 3+2/4). This is because singers added two additional morae (voids: ø) to the rhythm. These two voids are non-metrical pulses in time.

Rhythmic morae:	1 2	3 4	5 6	7 8	9 10
	La mie	tuu-vin	tyt-tö	las- ø	ta, ø
Metric morae:	1 2	3 4	5 6	7	8

The following Example A is in 2/4, but if singers add one pulse after two last poetic morae, the rhythm changes to 2+3/4 = 5/4 (Example B) without changing the poetic metre. Because of this, the last two syllables receive stress and can be sung as crotchets.

Quite a different approach is shown in Example C, in which the last tone of each measure is lengthened. Obviously the singer sung a crotchet during the fermata instead of a quaver, rendering the metre into 5/8. This simple change in musical timing creates a specific atmosphere.

There also are different ways to handle triple time and its derivatives. For example, it was customary to use 6/8 with minor stresses on odd-numbered syllables. Old Karelian wedding tunes have a specific character because of their treatment of musical metre. It is possible to encounter, say, a tune in 3/8+2/4 or in 3/8+7/8.

The singers decorated their songs in various rhythmic ways, but what is clear is that underlying all songs there is one basic scheme: the metric pattern of the poem with 4 stressed and 4 unstressed positions. If a singer stressed a syllable in an unstressed position (or vice versa), the effect was pleasing to the listener as it breaks the expected rule in a satisfactory way.

3 The mictic character of the runo disappears

The most ancient modal constructions (the mictic and the natural-tone based) began to change during the 2nd millennium AD. Influences came from the Christian world both East and West: Slavic and Western innovations began to mould the mictic character of the ancient runo modalities.

Slavic populations

One reason for this was the arrival of eastern Slavic populations, whose Proto-Slavic songs began to influence Karelian and Ingrian songs from the 10th century AD. One result of this was a preference for root VI (corresponding to the Dorian mode), which was only seldom found in Baltic-Finnic song.

St. Petersburg was founded in the middle of Ingria in the early 18th century. As late as in the early 20th century, there were still Finnish-speaking regions to the east of St. Petersburg where root VI was prominent in the *runo* songs. Generally speaking, when adopting Slavic idioms, Karelian singers began to migrate from their mictic grammar to a fully hexatonal grammar.

Western European tunes

Western European influences are apparent in that among *runo* melodies there are numerous dance tunes, Medieval ballads of Finnish and international origin, and later dance songs that were traditionally performed mainly by young people at church festivals, at work, at evening parties or at village festivals.

These song-dances in *runo* style were gradually replaced by figure dances and pair dances such as the *polska*, the *march* and the *mazurka*, mainly accompanied on the fiddle since the early 18th century. However, there are also tunes that clearly echo the repertoire of itinerant Medieval minstrels.

The Christian Middle Ages

The third cause of changes to *runo* melodies was the dominance of the Catholic Church in the Middle Ages (c. 1150–1520). In pagan Europe, it was customary everywhere for peasants to have spring rituals for magical reasons to promote the fertility of their fields and cattle. The Church began at an early date to harness these powerful rituals and turn them into Christian festivals.

This happened in Finland too: for instance, the procession of maidens who sang calendar songs at Whitsuntide was led by a priest carrying a cross. The songs belonging to this ritual clearly suggest that they were composed by learned men in the Middle Ages for the specific purpose of transforming the Dionysian fertility rites into a Christian event. In southern Finland, these songs were called *helkavirsi*, a conflation of the old Swedish word *hælgon* ('holy') and the Finnish word *virsi* ('sung spell'), which goes back to Neolithic times.

Root III

The fourth process to cause profound changes in the structure and aesthetics of *runo* melodies was the rising popularity of root III in Sweden, and soon in Finland too. When and how this happened, and why, is not known; and this ascendancy perhaps did not happen until the 17th century. (In terms of tonal vocabulary, root III is the harmonic minor lacking the 6th degree and having the dominant as its fundamental.)

It is obvious that the Finns adopted this root in the *runo* tradition along with the formal novelty of organizing four lines into one musical stanza. Moreover, alliteration — a feature typical of Finno-Ugric poetry in general — began to give way to rhyme as a structural device.

Quite a large number of *runo* tunes in Finland are based on root III. This clearly represents a recent shift in modal thinking. For instance, the oldest musical transcriptions of these melodies date from the late 18th century, representing this modality. It was the modality favoured by the upper classes in choosing *runo* tunes for school books and for published collections of music. The melodies were strophic by structure, the poetry tended to be rhymed, and the compass of the melodies could be up to an octave. All this satisfied the sensibilities of the educated Finns, who then proceeded to harmonize the tunes in harmonic minor.

This approach was opposed as early as in the late 19th century by **Jean Sibelius** (1865–1957), who had had direct contact with the oral tradition because of his encounters with Karelian singers. Sibelius was not understood; the specific nature of *runo* melodies was no longer known. The conventional wisdom was that *runo* songs were based on a major or minor pentachord and that the sort of tune shown in the following example is a typical *runo* tune.

The ancient origins of Finnish runo melodies

The most recent research shows that Finland was populated by Glacial Paleo-European groups advancing northwards from what today is southern Ukraine beginning in c. 14,000 BC. These people imported their Paleo-European song grammar to the area of Finland and Karelia around 10,000 BC. This grammar, or set of musical rules, was not as archaic as that of contemporary western Europeans who at the time were living in the area of northern Germany and would soon progress towards the northernmost coast of Norway, but it seems to have been widespread among the Mesolithic populations of eastern Europe.

Evidently populations living to the south and east of the Baltic Sea were already speaking an early variant of Proto-Finno-Ugric at the time, typified by words ending in a vowel and stress falling on the first syllable. It is also obvious that in pre-*runo* songs the lines were already organized with an even number of morae; linguistic evidence suggests that the line-with-eight-morae structure may have emerged in an even more remote past.

However, the appearance of the number eight in this context does not conclusively show that the trochaic tetrameter of *runo* song could have existed before the latter part of the 2nd millennium BC; also, the number of vowels in a line varied freely and extensively. Whatever happened in the area of present-day Finland and Estonia after the Stone Age, the fact remains that the song grammar of these early dwellers formed the foundation of later Baltic-Finnic song styles.

LAPPLAND

SWEDEN

DVINA

KARELIA

OLONEC

FINLAND

EAST

LADOGA

RUSSIA

WEST

ISTHMUS

LAKE
LADOGA

CITY OF TURKU

CITY OF ST. PETERSBURG

BALTIC SEA

INGRIA

ESTONIA

THE MAIN DISTRIBUTION OF RUNO SONG DURING THE EARLY 20TH CENTURY. KARELIA IS DIVIDED INTO DVINA KARELIA, OLENEC KARELIA (AUNUS), LADOGA KARELIA AND THE KARELIAN ISTHMUS, WHICH ALL LIE IN RUSSIA. THE INGRIANS (IZHORS) TO THE EAST OF THE ESTONIANS ARE A DISTINCT PEOPLE WHO SEPARATED FROM THE PROTO-KARELIANS.

II Kalevala poetry in Finnish folk music

Timo Leisiö:

THE RUNO CODE. THE FINNISH EPIC FOLK SONG TRADITION IN FINLAND

The *Kalevala* is composed of epic folk songs written down in Karelia, Ingria and Finland during the first part of the 19th century. The collecting of these independent folk songs has continued up to our time, and the present article briefly outlines some of their features.

It is impossible to understand the Baltic-Finnic *runo* tradition (i.e. the tradition of the Finns, Karelians, Estonians and other peoples living to the east of the Baltic Sea) without keeping in mind that it was only transmitted orally from generation to generation by singing. Each *runo* poem existed in the individual memories of people, and the seeming stability of their themes and contents in fact conceals a continuous process of change.

1 Principal categories

In ancient times, there were three main categories of song in Finnish and Karelian folk culture: the lament *(itku)*, the hallooing *(huikkaus)*, and finally the *runo*, being the most elementary feature of the Finnish poetry.

Laments and hallooing

Laments were performed at two major junctures of farewell: the wedding ritual at the home of a bride and the funeral ritual at the home and the grave of a deceased person. *Wedding laments* were performed by the mother or the sister of the bride, her maiden friends and expert women who specialized in lamenting.

WITH THE NATIONAL ROMANTIC MOVEMENT, RUNO SINGERS CAME TO BE TREATED WITH A NEARLY WORSHIPFUL REVERENCE. THIS SUBTLE IMAGE OF *Teppana Jänis* FROM 1916 CAPTURES A NUMBER OF MOTIFS: AN OLD MAN MUCH LIKE VÄINÄMÖINEN SITTING IN A BOAT CONCENTRATING ON HIS KANTELE, SURROUNDED BY AN ALMOST ARCHETYPAL FINNISH LANDSCAPE. PHOTO: FINNISH LITERATURE SOCIETY.

Death laments were performed by the close female relatives of the deceased. In Karelia, women also lamented when taking leave of their sons who went to fight in the Russian army. Sometimes people (even men) sang laments on unexpected occasions such as encountering a dear friend or saying farewell to an honoured guest. Such laments were improvised on the spot. Lamenting was forbidden in Lutheran Finland, but it was still alive and well in Greek Orthodox Karelia and Ingria in the 20th century.

The second main genre, hallooing *(huikkaus)*, involved the singing of melodic calls in a high register to contact people and domesticated animals for instance in the forest.

Embracing life as a whole: the runo code

In all other cases, it was the *runo* pattern into which all emotional expression and rational knowledge was musically cast, well into the 17th century. The existence of a single code covering the vast majority of expression in culture, from children's lore to sacred knowledge, was most unusual in Europe in ancient times, yet this was the situation in Finland and Karelia as recently as two to four centuries ago.

Nearly everything could be sung in the *runo* code, i.e. the iterative metric pattern of eight *morae* often performed with mictic melodies (see page x). It was by listening to these songs that children learned about the creation of the world, the first boat, the first fire or the first psaltery *(kantele)*. The magical knowledge to heal the sick and wounded, to protect the cattle from wolves and bears or to control the wind and fire also used the runic code. It was used to sing chants to transport the soul of a hunted and killed bear back to its celestial home, the constellation of the Great Bear. It was used for love songs, songs of sorrow, songs of longing and loss, tales of adventure, lullabies, children's songs and mocking songs. There were not very many war songs in Finland and Karelia, but even those were sung in the *runo* code.

The reason for this widespread use of the *runo* code is simple. Its metric pattern was optimal for the Finnic languages, and it was easy for people to remember poems in this style and to improvise new ones.

2 Singing the runo poems

Singers, seers and shamans

It used to be the case that to sing was not to perform but to communicate. People used to sing on fishing journeys, when spinning or weaving a net, or when rowing a boat or doing some other mechanic work. No wonder, then, that even small children quickly learned the code and the songs themselves, and there are reports of children improvising with ease for more than an hour when lulling a baby.

Because of the magical functions of *runo* texts, people with a good memory and talent as a seer were respected. Formerly, the verb *laulaa* ('to sing' or 'to enchant by singing') was treated as transitive in the same way as the modern Sámi word *juoi'kat* ('to yoik or sing [someone]'). This is how Väinämöinen *"sang Jouka-hainen in a marsh up to his belt, he sang Joukahainen's dog, with its claws in a cold rock – [and his] arrow to a hawk streaking high in the heavens --"*. Singers might have singing contests, which were great fun for observers: two men took turns singing until one of them ran out of repertoire.

Naturally, people admired singers with beautiful voices. However, the greatest respect was afforded to singers with a good memory and supreme command of powerful spells that were needed for healing the sick or wounded and for solving practical problems (such as finding lost cattle or property). 19th-century reports indicate that the most highly respected 'singers' were often seers and healers with no musical talent. Known as *tietäjät* ('wise men', literally 'knowers'), these were the successors of the ancient shamans. The educated scholars of the late 19th century were thus at cross purposes with the local people when asking after 'good singers', because what the scholars expected to find were of course good singers of epic and lyrical poems.

The transformation of shamanism to the magical practice of the wise men seems to have been slow. It is possible that the more shamanism declined, the less frequently spells were performed by singing. The shamans slowly retreated inland to the northeast from the coastal southwestern. Evidently there was some shamanic activity in central Finland as late as in the 16th and 17th centuries.

Call and response

Because all the *runo* poems were memorized and each person remembered them in a personal way, at social occasions such as the bear ritual there was (usually) one man in social feasts singing the story. Each poetic line he sang was repeated by the others with more or less variation on the melody. There was no singing in parts, except among young people in the Isthmus of Karelia in the 19th century, a device borrowed from Russian culture.

It could also happen in Finland that two men sat hand in hand opposite to each other. One of them was the principal singer, and the other one repeated each of his lines. This style of singing seems also to have been a feature of social functions but was not a rule because it was a performance, which excluded everyone else present from the pleasant occupation of singing.

Individual differences in remembering the 'same' story also made it difficult for people to sing a poem simultaneously together. This led to the call-and-response practice: a leader sang a line which the others then repeated in chorus. This had the effect of giving the leader a moment to plan the next line to make the presentation as interesting as possible. In other words, the practice helped the solo singer to be artistically creative. It is quite possible that the emergence of the 5/4 metre happened because the lengthening of the last two *morae* into two double *morae* gave the solo singer more time to think about the next line (see p. 34).

In the Karelian Isthmus, it was also customary especially for young maidens to sing group songs with the chorus repeating a refrain instead of the previous line. This seems to have been a practice borrowed from the Russians, and these refrains sometimes contained corrupted Russian words.

The art of a thousand variants

In any one area, the local people only used a few melodies. Therefore, people sung lots of different kinds of poems using only a few tunes. The concept of melody was different from what we understand as melody today: a melody was simply a basic pattern that functioned as a starting point for an improvisation. From sound recordings, we know that in olden times singers could vary a pattern in any number of ways rhythmically, melodically, by intensity and by voice production, turning one song into one thousand. There was a great deal of freedom.

For instance, the tune in Example 1 is one transcribed by Jean Sibelius. It was sung by two singers, and Sibelius identified some 50 variants of their double lines, "all based on this melody". **Heikki Laitinen** (b. 1943) analyzed the same story sung by another singer 60 years later, in 1952; the song contained 66 double lines, all different in tune and treatment of metre (in both text and melody).

EXAMPLE 1. THE MEDIEVAL LEGEND OF VIRGIN MARY AND THE MYSTERIOUS BIRTH OF CHRIST, AS TRANSCRIBED BY **Jean Sibelius** ON HIS HONEYMOON IN KARELIA IN 1892. FIRST PUBLISHED BY **Erik Tawaststjerna** (1988, 22) AND NOW DEPOSITED IN THE HELSINKI UNIVERSITY LIBRARY.

There are only a few *runo* poems associated with a specific tune. Karelian wedding tunes are a case in point. There may have been some ritual songs that were sung to a specific tune, at least locally, but the general view among researchers despite a shortage of data is that almost any poem could be sung with any melody.

Tradition and change in former societies

From the Stone Age onwards (before the emergence of the runo code), Proto-Finnic men might adopt new cultural elements while visiting the Ural Mountains or present-day Poland or Denmark during the winter. Returning to their families, they enriched their local culture with what they had learned. The women took care of children, but even though they 'stayed at home', each of them made one major move in their lives: when getting married, a woman might move dozens or hundreds of kilometres from her home village to the home of her husband. (It might also happen that a man moved in with the family of his bride.)

What is important is that, even in the 2nd millennium AD, cultural elements could become diffused over a wide area and that on the other hand it was the woman who, in a natural way, conveyed *her* family culture to her children in both uniethnic and biethnic marriages. As a result, any local culture was run by the powers of preservation and renewal. A woman who learned the mictic grammar (see p. x) in her childhood taught it to her children, and this led to a cultural merger in a society where this grammar did not previously exist.

All this worked in favour of the runo tradition. Until the 16th century and even later, most of Finland and Karelia consisted of regions loosely controlled by people who shared a local sense of unity, for instance because of a common dialect. There was no centralized world view, religion or conception of art. Each region was divided into small local societies, consisting of villages and families. People might travel vast distances when trading, hunting or fishing, but there was much local variation even if the body of *runo* poetry and melody was largely uniform.

3 Genres of runo poetry

Researchers have divided the *runo* poems into numerous genres and larger units such as the epic and lyric poems, wedding songs, work and calendar songs, magical spells, and even proverbs (which were not sung). However, in reality, singers often combined various kinds of theme in one song, and thus a song could belong to various genres. In other words, a song could simultaneously contain elements from various lyrical and epic sources.

Epic poems

There are hundreds of epic *runo* poems. Most of them were local, but dozens of them were widely known and sung; these are the poems that also form the basis of the *Kalevala* — the *Forging of the Sky* by the celestial smith, Ilmarinen, otherwise known as Ukko 'Old Man', the Thunder God; *The Spell*, the tale of Väinämöinen's visit to the grave of a deceased shaman; or *The Visit to Tuonela*, a description of the shaman Väinämöinen travelling to the Underworld in a trance in search of knowledge. In one way or another, these songs seem to have been a part of a Stone Age shamanic ritual.

Lemminkäinen is a reminiscence of Finnic shamanism in which shamans could easily become enemies. In this tale, the shaman meets his enemy Väinämöinen at the *Päivölä* banquet and gets killed. This song was a great favourite. There also are songs such as *Sun and Moon, The Bond, The Incest, The Bear, The Oak, The Great Ox, The Elk and The Sower,* which all date back to pre-Christian times and to societies based on totemic organisations.

Catholic priests (who mostly came from among the common people) knew these poems and also created new ones to turn pagan mentalities and ethics towards Christianity from around the 13th century. In the Middle Ages, the Finns began to adopt a wholly new epic tradition, that of western European ballads, which were translated into Finnish using the runo code. The last popular songs to be composed in this code date from the 18th century, being concerned with specific occurrences of the then most recent war and the political history of Sweden-Finland.

Väinämöinen rides his blue deer

The ancient singers often combined various kinds of theme in one song. A good example of this practice is a *runo* about Väinämöinen on a journey, riding his "blue deer". In this *runo*, a Lapp shaman shoots the deer, whereupon the rider falls into the sea and finds himself in big trouble. The story then goes on. The introduction is actually about a Sámi shaman who shot the Power Animal of the Finnic shaman Väinämöinen with his magical means. Väinämöinen was riding his deer in order to find the missing 'words' needed to complete the creation of the world's first boat.

The rest of this 'adventure' contains two cosmogonic myths. One of them is the myth of the diving bird living in the non-luminous Proto-Ocean. It dives to the bottom of the ocean and collects the elements for the creation. The other myth is that of the Proto-Bird, living in the open Proto-Sea, which lays several eggs on the knees of Väinämöinen (who is resting in the sea); out of these eggs the universe was created. In this song, it is thus Väinämöinen himself who is the Creator.

Understanding this song has been the focus of much study. Its elements date back deep into the Stone Age, and from this point of view the complexity of the tune, shifting from the hexatonal grammar to the mictic one, creates an archaic atmosphere.

Natural tones 8-12 of the Primary Pillar on G.   Natural tones 6-12 of the Pillar on A.

THE BEGINNING OF A MYTHICAL SONG FROM DVINA KARELIA ABOUT THE SHAMAN VÄINÄMÖINEN WHO FALLS INTO THE SEA.

Lyrical songs and the genre of 'personal songs'

Looking at the 'lyrical' songs, we encounter the same problem as in epic songs. The genres defined by outside analysts are both appropriate and inappropriate. Lyrical songs cover all branches of the everyday life of ancient Finns. **Senni Timonen** (b. 1944), in her profound analysis of *runo* lyrics, made it clear that a notable number of lyrical songs concern personal histories.

From the global point of view, this means that the circumpolar genre of the 'personal song', so prominent in Sámi, Samoyedic and Amerindian cultures, was still present in the runo tradition (from which Elias Lönnrot fashioned his lyrical poetry collection, the *Kanteletar*, see p. 29). Quite a few of them were either traditional or new songs about the fate of a widow, daughter, daughter-in-law, sister-in-law, mistreated wife, etc., related in first-person narrative.

The Baltic-Finnic lament is a stylistic continuation of the archaic genre of personal song. However, numerous *runo* lullabies and lyrical songs also intersect the lament in certain points, and each of these can thus represent the underlying genre of the 'personal song'.

Songs to entertain

There also is a vast number of entertainment songs for children, sung by adults while lulling a baby or doing their daily routines. These are amusing, humorous, close to the animal world and often absurd, which can be partly explained by their connections with the ancient myths and shamanic lore.

One sub-genre here is that of chain poems, which contain elements that are so archaic that they must have been known for thousands of years. One of the most effective is where a child describes his/her nightmare. It is related as a series of frightening occurrences that follow one another breathlessly, as if in an action film: "*[The bad one] killed my ma, my pa, my five brothers, seven of my uncle's children, and it wanted to kill me, too; I climbed up on a fence, the fence fell on a rock, the rock split in two, I jumped to a fir tree, the fir tree burst in six pieces, flamed up in seven torches --*". There were also lots of songs sung by both adults and children.

Calendar songs

There were calendar-linked spring and local festivals (such as parish and church holidays) which had songs of their own. For instance, St. George's Day and the Whitsuntide were celebrated with processions and the magic of fertility. It was usually the women who were responsible for this. There are quite a few recorded erotic songs; in these calendar rituals they were sung by women amongst themselves. In springtime, young people performed dance songs; in winter, dancing could only be done in private homes, because of which there were also songs for asking permission to dance and finally for thanking the host. There were songs for social games played by everyone in the evenings; songs for calendar festivals; all kinds of mocking songs; songs of women, boys and men; songs of love and of social relations (such as those between children and parents); songs of advice for young men and maidens; and songs about the local area. There was an extensive group of songs belonging to the wedding ritual, and there were also pastoral songs and other types of work song.

'Spell of Iron'

O thou poor pathetic iron,

Thou wert not too whole or handsome

When as milk thou still wert hiding

In the breasts of one young maiden!

From the bog then thou wert lifted,

From the rock then thou wert blasted!

Busy bee, O tiny birdling,

Bring us honey from the forest,

Bring us mead now from the woodland,

Bring it us to heal the wounding,

Bring it us to cure the damage!

In the holy name of Jesus!

The 'Spell of Iron': material spanning four and a half millennia

Among the genres of *runo* poetry, a surprisingly large one is that of spells, chants used to normalize all kinds of crises and to achieve various things (such as to cure impotence or to drive harmful insects away). Sometimes a spell contains lines that draw a cultural panorama across many millennia. This *Spell of Iron* from the 18th century was used when stopping the blood and healing a wound made by an axe. Naturally, the wise men did not know the historical background of their knowledge. However, analyzed from the point of view of our present knowledge, the text reveals astonishing things.

The first four lines go back to a widespread belief that iron originated in the World Tree where four maidens (or a cow or a goat) were living. From their breasts came four rivers of milk which spread iron all around the world. The next two lines refer to the primitive techniques of gathering iron ore from the bottom of lakes and bogs, as practiced in Finland from the early Iron Age (c. 500 BC onwards).

Then comes a request to the bee to bring forth honey and mead to cure the wound. This takes us to the steppes of southern Russia, populated by Indo-Aryan nomads who domesticated the bee and made mead, both incorporated into their mythology — as we know from Sanskrit mythology. The reference to the bee would seem to date back to late Proto-Finno-Ugric, the early Proto-Aryan era some 4,000 years ago. It is also highly likely that the first elements of the reference to milk as the ultimate origin of iron (or copper) also goes back to this constellation of early cultures — even if the Finns did re-adopt this tradition from the Proto-Germans later. In other words, these lines can be read as follows in terms of pinpointing the chronology and points of population contact:

Lines 1-2:	*c. 500 BC–*	*Baltic Sea coasts*
Lines 3-4	*c. 2500 BC – 300 AD*	*Southern Russian steppes and Southern Scandinavia*
Lines 5-6	*c. 300 BC–*	*Central Sweden and Finland*
Lines 7-11	*c. 3000–2000 BC*	*Southern Russian steppes (Indo-Aryan Abashevo Complex)*
Line 12	*c. 1200 AD*	*Catholic Southwest Finland*

Even if the dates are rough estimates, this demonstrates that the Finns and the Karelians carried a wealth of knowledge in their oral tradition.

4 The broken code of runo poetry

'Rekilaulu' confuses the runo: the arrival of European popular music culture

There is no doubt that the *Kalevala* was a factor in the people of Finland, including the Swedish-speaking Finns, gaining a specific Finnish national identity. However, it is also a fact that before the 19th century the common people in both town and country had little respect for the ancient *runo* tradition. The songs were regarded as old-fashioned and uninteresting.

Instead, a new lyric song tradition known as *rekilaulu* ('round-dance song', literally 'sleigh song') was developed. It was partly based on the *runo* code in 5/4 metre, but organized into rhymed four-line stanzas following models of central European and Scandinavian origin. This genre was used for instance by young men when asking permission from maidens to visit them at night — part of the socially controlled night-courting customs in southern Finland. It was also favoured when singing mocking songs, love songs or songs of social protest, or when dancing with no fiddler available. It is amazing how far the mictic grammar (see p. 33) persisted in these 19th-century songs.

The runo code in the modern world

Singing is about communicating emotions. With the Finns and the Karelians, this means that the *runo* code was never just about trochaic tetrameter, as scholars usually baldly describe it. The code was highly esteemed as a poetic vehicle by the Finns for more than two millennia from the late Bronze Age onwards. Then came the breakdown.

One reason for the breakdown was the Lutheran Church, which fought the *runo* code by criminalizing it. The style was banned in the 16th and 17th centuries. In the 17th century, the King of Sweden-Finland realized that the unwritten history of the realm could be found in folklore, and priests began to write down stories and songs in both Sweden and Finland. However, by now the Finns had grown wary, and the *runo* style began to decline — although the scarcity of doctors and hospitals meant that the spells of the seers survived as an underground tradition as far as into the 20th century.

Today, Finns are not particularly fascinated in the *Kalevala* or the old *runo* poetry. The main reason both for this and the extinct of the runo folk culture is the loss of the code: the textual code is still vaguely known and appreciated but the musical code, the social contexts, and the old world view and its values have been irretrievably lost.

The *runo* code, then, was a unitary system. Without music, the *Kalevala* remains a good deal more abstract for a modern Finn than the original folk poems sung in the form of 'world music'. However, the world music boom cannot make the *runo* code return — there is no way to restore the world view that is a thing of the past. The loss of *runo* music is the loss of its grammar, and the loss of its grammar is the loss of a social structure, an identity and a system of values. We may touch them through research, but only rarely can we experience them emotionally. The emotions communicated by archaic *runo* melodies cannot easily be encoded by modern-day Finns.

Although much has been lost, the *runo* lore is not completely extinct. There are local groups and individuals who keep the tradition alive by studying it in the archives. Using the tradition in popular music and in new folk music is a recent trend. The tradition also inspires classical composers. All this suggests that there is a distinct determination to keep the tradition alive through re-interpretation and through giving it new meanings and messages. But even apart from this, the *runo* tradition is unconsciously known to modern Finns, and the code is repeated in such applications as advertisements because of its aesthetic qualities. The code is equally well known to Swedish-speaking Finns, and it was one of them, Jean Sibelius, who provided a strong impulse for uniting the Swedish-speaking and Finnish-speaking cultures in Finland by combining Karelian and Scandinavian elements of folklore into his individual symphonic style, often considered very much Finnish.

Timo Leisiö & Helena Ruhkala:

THE KANTELE. FROM THE JAW OF A PIKE TO ELECTRIC AMPLIFICATION

The origins of the kantele

In runo songs, there are two myths about the origin of *kantele*, the Baltic psaltery with 5 strings. The eastern one is related to the Mediterranean myths of *Singing Orpheus* and the *Lyre of Apollo*. The western one is related to the Celtic myth about the invention of the first lyre, the *crwth*, which was made of the bones and sinews of a huge fish. The latter was usually connected to the Finnic variant of singing Orpheus in which it is clearly pronounced that the inventor of the *kantele*, Väinämöinen, "both sang and played".

In ancient times, the *kantele* was mainly played by one player who improvised a never-ending continuum of melodic configurations. Typical of the style was that a player never stopped a string but let it sound until he touched it the next time. The instrument was rarely used to accompany songs. The Finnic peoples with their mictic grammar (based on fusing prepentatonic elements with hexatonal ones) had difficulties with harmonic thinking. What this means is that it was not usual to play while singing or to sing while playing. We know that sometimes a soloist (telling the story) was accompanied by a *kantele* player who repeated the melodic line of the soloist in one way or another. Only a few transcriptions have survived.

There are data suggesting other practices too. Sometimes a singer played what he sung, except that once in a while he also plucked a dichord. Sometimes a singer used a specific modal root while the accompanying *kantele* was tuned to another root.

>>> THE SIMPLE FIVE-STRING VERSION OF THE KANTELE UNDERSCORES THE PENTATONIC NATURE OF ANCIENT FINNISH RUNO SINGING. THE KANTELE IS USED IN MUSIC EDUCATION IN SOME SCHOOLS, AS IT IS EXCELLENT FOR SIMPLE CHORDAL ACCOMPANIMENTS. PHOTO: TIMO VILLANEN.

In the 19th century, the *kantele* became the symbol of the Finnish nationalist movement. It was featured in the poetry of the *Kalevala* and the *Kanteletar*, it was depicted in the works of painters, and *kantele* players and *runo* singers were invited to appear, as emissaries of the past, at song and music festivals organized to propagate the nationalist movement. The *kantele* remains the national instrument to this day.

From hollowed-out wood to amplification

The oldest types of kantele had five strings and were hollowed out from a single piece of wood. In the early 19th century, the instrument acquired more strings, at which point its structure evolved into one made up of wood strips joined with wood spikes or glue.

In the 1920s, **Paul Salminen** (1887–1949) developed the 36-string concert *kantele* with a tuning mechanism and damper board. The tuning mechanism represented a milestone in the development of the instrument, since it enabled instantaneous re-tuning of the diatonic instrument by a semitone up or down.

The most recent significant development is the solid-wood, modern design 39-string electric *kantele* designed by **Hannu Koistinen** (b. 1966) in 1999. A range of small Wing *kantele* types with 5 to 15 strings was designed in its wake. The new electric and semi-acoustic *kantele* models are streamlined and have colour schemes resembling those of sports cars.

Koistinen's innovations have changed the position in which the instrument is played and, at the same

THE NEW ELECTRIC KANTELES BY **Hannu Koistinen** HAVE RESHAPED THE IMAGE OF FINLAND'S NATIONAL INSTRUMENT. THE TRADITIONAL WOODEN INSTRUMENT HAS TURNED INTO A COLOURFUL AND TRENDY DESIGN PIECE. PHOTO: TIMO VILLANEN.

time, the nature of performances on the *kantele*. The Wing models are the first mass-produced instruments that come equipped with a shoulder strap, enabling the performer to move more freely during the performance. Instead of being played horizontally on a table top as per tradition, the 39-string electric *kantele* is tilted forward, so that the audience has a better view of the player's fingers and the strings of the instrument.

In terms of sound, the most important change is that the built-in microphones enable the entire range of the instrument to be balanced without changing the authentic sound. Suitable for both clubs and stadiums, this futuristic high-tech instrument has attracted wide interest in all kinds of musical genres.

Changing and adapting kantele repertoire

For centuries, the *kantele* was an instrument used mainly in traditional music. The tunes played on small types of *kantele* included imitations of church bells, *runo* tunes and dance tunes such as *maanitus* or *trepak*. Continuous rhythmic, melodic and harmonic variation on the detail level has always been typical of the performance style. Polyphony has also been typical ever since the earliest days of the five-string *kantele*.

Improvements in the technical properties of the *kantele* have increased its use and its potential. In recent decades, composers have begun to make use of fla-geolets, double flageolets, stopped notes and other imaginative ways of playing. These developments were pioneered primarily by Professor **Martti Pokela** (b. 1924).

In the early 20th century, arrangements for the concert *kantele* were usually based on folk songs; but in the late 20th century, many Finnish composers such as **Kalevi Aho** (b. 1949), **Pekka Jalkanen** (b. 1945), **Pehr Henrik Nordgren** (b. 1944) and **Toivo Kärki** (1915–1992) began to write solo works, chamber music and orchestral music for the *kantele*. The effect modules and looping devices that can be hooked up to the electric *kantele* have opened up new sound colour possibilities. **Timo Väänänen** (b. 1970) was one of the first performers on the electric kantele. He has released a disc of music for the electric kantele, *Matka — Voyage* (2001), and he frequently gives recitals in Finland and abroad.

Further reading

Hannu Saha: *The Kantele – from Epic to Eclecticism*
www.fimic.fi > Folk and World Music > Articles

Pekko Käppi:

ANCIENT VOICES IN THE FIRMAMENT OF NEW FOLK MUSIC

The term 'new folk music' in Finland refers broadly to the new approach to traditional music-making that began to emerge in the 1980s, focusing on the newly-founded Folk Music Department of the Sibelius Academy. Although we might say that the Finnish new folk music boom is still in its infancy — compared with the decade-long hegemony of Irish folk music, for example — many Finnish artists have already established an international career for themselves. Several bands and artists such as **Värttinä, JPP, Maria Kalaniemi** (b. 1963), **Wimme** (b. 1959), **MeNaiset, Suden Aika, Helsinki Mandoliners, Gjallarhorn** and **Kimmo Pohjonen** (b. 1964) tour the world regularly.

There is something of a boom in the popularity enjoyed by these Finnish artists. They are generously noted by the media, and their concerts are well attended. Finnish discs licensed or released by international record labels are distributed and sold worldwide. Moreover, Finnish folk musicians collaborate with leading international artists and producers.

Old texts and Lönnrot methods

Although instrumental music holds a strong presence in Finnish new folk music, there is also a considerable body of music drawing on the song traditions of the Finns, the Karelians, the Sámi and the Swedish-speaking Finns. Song is an integral solo component in the music of Värttinä, Wimme, MeNaiset, Suden Aika and Gjallarhorn, for example.

Värttinä, MeNaiset and Suden Aika in particular have promoted the most idiosyncratic branch of the Finnish song tradition, *Kalevala* singing or *runo* singing. An important text source in their music is the monumental collection *Suomen Kansan Vanhat Runot* (Ancient Poetry of the Finnish People), a 34-volume compendium compiled between 1908 and 1997. It complements the canonized poems of the *Kalevala* in many ways.

Nevertheless, Lönnrot's method of combining scraps of poetry into a continuous narrative is alive and well among new folk singers. **Mari Kaasinen** (b. 1971) of Värttinä, for instance, has explained in interviews that she writes her songs surrounded by volumes of the Ancient Poetry collection, combining bits of poems as her fancy strikes her. New folk musicians tend to choose lyrical and 'moody' poems and spells, with the occasional foray into epic themes.

The new folk musicians take even more liberties with *runo* melodies. Melodic elements are often derived from Ingrian and Karelian tunes, and Värttinä for example has drawn on Fenno-Ugric song traditions of various kinds, such as the polyphonic singing of the Mari and the Setu people or of the Hungarians, combining these with *Kalevala* poetry.

Burlakat, a band which like Värttinä originated from the village of Rääkkylä in eastern Finland, has been promoting singing in the Karelian language and has embarked on a conquest of Europe courtesy of a license deal signed with the German label Humppa Records.

Värttinä and the Finnish woman's blues

The internationally most successful Finnish new folk music band drawing on the *Kalevala* tradition is Värttinä. The band has traced a spectacular career from a youth group in an obscure North Karelian village to the ranks of world music stardom.

Sanna Kurki-Suonio (b. 1966) and **Tellu Turkka** (b. 1969) have pursued a rough-hewn and contrast-laden interpretation of *Kalevala* singing. Both on disc and in concert, their deep and beautiful voices of the singers escalate at times into an anarchist shaman act. They both sang with the Swedish band **Hedningarna** in the 1990s but have also released acclaimed solo albums entitled *Musta* (Black, Kurki-Suonio) and *Suden aika* (Time of the Wolf, Turkka).

Tellu Turkka and **Liisa Matveinen** (b. 1962) have also scored something of a success abroad with the disc *Mateli*, based on the poetry of runo singer **Mateli**

Kuivalatar (1771–1846) of Ilomantsi — the disc has been described as "Finnish woman's blues". The Suden Aika quartet headed by these two women has appeared frequently abroad, for instance in Germany, where they, like Burlakat, released their latest album, *Etsijä* (Seeker). Turkka and Matveinen appeared with contemporary *runo* singer **Taito Hoffrén** (b. 1974) on the disc *Runolaulutanssit* (Poem song dance) of the **Tallari** band, where ancient poetry meets Finnish tango and foxtrot.

MeNaiset has been pioneering Finnish new folk music in polyphonic form for over a decade. It has a more tradition-conscious approach to the poetry than Värttinä: the band's first disc includes painstaking bibliographical notes for all the poetry, for example. The band has toured internationally and collaborated with the Mordvin ensemble **Toorama**. MeNaiset has released two discs, *MeNaiset* and *Mastorava*.

The heyday of ancient groove

Although the principal hero of the *Kalevala*, Väinämöinen, accompanied his singing on the kantele, the runo tradition mainly involved unaccompanied singing. New folk music, however, incorporates any number of instrumentations.

Old Finnish folk instruments have been part and parcel of the tool kit of new folk musicians from the very first. The kantele, jouhikko, liru, mänkeri, jaw harp, various horns and flutes rub shoulders with more conventional instruments.

Improvisation is also an essential part of new folk music. One of the pioneers of improvisation in this field and also one of the longest-lived new folk music ensembles apart from Värttinä is **The World Mänkeri Orchestra** (formerly **EtnoPojat**), who have released a dozen discs. They specialize in constructing ancient Finnish wind instruments, liru and mänkeri, and have also pursued innovations.

The year 2003 saw the publication of the world's first disc of jouhikko (the bowed lyre) music, *Hiien Hivuksista – Jouhikko Music from Finland*. It brought together ten Finnish jouhikko players in a variety of ensembles, performing both repertoire from the past and new compositions.

Thanks to a diverse range of training and research in folk music, the genre is enjoying increasing popularity in Finland. More and more people are taking up folk music in an increasing variety of forms. The ancient and idiosyncratic groove of the Finnish musical tradition is perhaps now stronger than ever.

Select discography

* *Hiien Hivuksista – Jouhikko Music from Finland* (2003).
Folk Music Institute KICD 82.
* *The Kalevala Heritage* (1995).
Archive recordings of ancient Finnish songs. ODE 849-2.
* **Kurki-Suonio, Sanna:** *Musta* (1998).
Zen Garden GAR, North Side USA NSD 6021.
* **Matveinen, Liisa & Virkkala [Turkka], Tellu:** *Mateli* (1999).
Folk Music Institute KICD 64.
* **MeNaiset:** *MeNaiset* (1995). Folk Music Institute KICD 37.
* **MeNaiset:** *Mastorava* (2001). MNCD 1.
* **Suden aika:** *Suden aika / Etsijä* (2004).
Alba NCD 24, Laika Germany 3510193.2.
* **Tellu [Turkka]:** *Suden aika* (1996). Folk Music Institute KICD 43.
* **Tellu, Liisa, Taito and Tallari:** *Runolaulutanssit* (2003).
Folk Music Institute KICD 80.
* **Värttinä.** See the Värttinä discography, p. 65.
* **The World Mänkeri Orchestra:** *Inky Joy* (2004).
Folk Music Institute KICD 90.

Harri Römpötti: *Värttinä*

Värttinä was born in 1983 in the tiny village of Rääkkylä, as a project of **Sari** (b. 1967) and **Mari Kaasinen** (b. 1971). The group eventually had as many as 21 members playing the kantele, singing and reciting Karelian poetry. Although the *runo* songs of Karelia still represent the very essence of the group's expertise, a lot has changed since the early days.

The evolution towards the recent line-up of Värttinä began in the late 1980's. There were fewer singers and elements of rock music were introduced. The album *Oi dai* marked a milestone not only for the group but for the whole Finnish folk music scene, making Värttinä steady favourites with rock club audiences and, indeed, the whole nation. Never before had folk music been this popular among young people.

Oi dai ended up selling platinum in Finland, but it also raised a lot of hackles, something that seems hard to believe today. Some folk musicians strongly disapproved of this modernised style that didn't fit their puristic, almost archival ideas of how the folk tradition should be preserved. The archives of their minds were still to be aired by the winds of world music.

Since then there certainly hasn't been any lack of fresh ideas on the Finnish folk music scene. Värttinä have played a big part in creating the general well-being and stylistic pluralism that today's folk music enjoys. Rääkkylä is well on its way to becoming a Kaustinen-style folk music hot spot.

The success of *Oi dai* eventually led the group to worldwide fame. For years now, Värttinä have been Finland's shiniest international world music stars, touring the world and performing side by side with superstars from all musical genres. With an excellent catalogue of albums, Värttinä are still at their best as a live act, continuing to deliver performances that burst with energy.

Not many bands would have been able to cope with the dramatic line-up changes that Värttinä have gone through. Not only is Värttinä still going strong, but they are maintaining a distinct stylistic continuity as well. With a mish-mash of multicultural ingredients enriching their sound, the brisk, bright singing of the women is still the centrepiece, celebrating the strong song tradition of Karelia.

Värttinä are now moving onto new, exiting territories. In collaboration with **A.R. Rahman,** one of the most successful Bollywood film music composers, Värttinä are in the process of composing original music for the musical stage presentation of **J.R.R. Tolkien's** *Lord of the Rings*, premiering in London in 2005.

Translated by Hanna-Mari Latham
(previously published in the *Arctic Paradise* catalogue, Fimic 2004)

Värttinä discography

Värttinä / The First Album (1987). Finlandia Innovator Series 0630-18062
Musta lindu / Black Bird (1989). Finlandia Innovator Series 3984-23229-2
Oi dai (1990). PolyGram Finland / SPIRITCD 4
Seleniko (1992). PolyGram Finland/SPIRIT 517467-2
Aitara (1994). MIPUCD 302
Kokko (1996). Nonesuch / Warner 79429-2
Vihma (1998). Wicklow / BMG 09026-63262-2
Ilmatar (2000). Wicklow / BMG 09026-63678-2
6.12. (live album, 2001). BMG 74321 881802 8
Double Life (compilation, 2002). Trees Music & Art Taiwan TMCD 313/314
iki (2003). BMG 74321 981452

>>> www.varttina.com

III

Kalevala poetry in Finnish classical music

Antti Häyrynen

1 Folk poetry in the service of the government

Interest in the literary and musical heritage of the Finnish people was kindled in the top echelons of society at an early date. A memorandum from the King of Sweden dated in 1630 exhorts the recording of folk tradition as testimony of a long and noble history.

From the very first, the substance of the *Kalevala* tradition was musically appropriated by the central government, and by high culture as its representative, for the purpose of shaping folk tradition as it suited them. As early as in the Reformation period there were efforts to adapt the '*Kalevala* culture' to the western world view, and the power and influence of pagan wise men and *runo* singers was viewed with much suspicion in the Lutheran Church (see p. 13). In the east, the Orthodox Church was much more relaxed and tolerant about this sort of thing, and as a result the ancient folk tradition survived in the wilds of Karelia up to the late 19th century.

The mandate from on high which governed the collecting and application of the *Kalevala* poetry lent a grandeur and nobility to any and all interpretations of the national epic, even when the original material contained nothing of the kind. There was a decided determination towards linking the national epic first to the culture of the realm and later to national culture, but these efforts were characterized by a curious dichotomy in attitudes: the material was viewed with both enthusiasm and censorship.

The great minds of the Enlightenment period, such as **Henrik Gabriel Porthan** (1739–1804), Professor at the Academy in Turku, who collected folk poetry and folk tunes, saw features of famous European mythological constructs reflected in the *Kalevala* material. On the other hand, Porthan shared the perception held by western culture (or, more specifically, by the Swedish-speaking elite) of Finnish people as slow, passive, dour and taciturn. This pervasive attitude found its way later into musical portraits of the common people too.

It is from Porthan that we get the stereotype of equating the folk poetry of the *Kalevala* with the Finnish national character: "These songs, all sung to the same tune, simple and serious like the people themselves, and accompanied when possible with a sort of harp — these songs were sung by women too, to while away their heavy work in milling grain." (1788)

2 "Finns have a sensitive affinity for music and poetry." Signor Acerbi visits the poetic people of the North

"But as soon as we began to play their *runo* tune, there was not a dry eye in the house, and the emotion was palpable. The *runo* is an ancient Finnish tune that lives on among the common people and has adapted itself to their national instrument."

Italian explorer **Giuseppe Acerbi** (1773–1846) spent two months in Oulu, the then northernmost town in Finland, in 1799. Oulu was home to Provincial Accountant **Erik Tulindberg** (1761–1814), also known as a violinist and a composer.

It was probably Tulindberg who introduced Acerbi to the kantele and to the *Kalevala* tunes which Acerbi then published in his travel book. Acerbi played the clarinet himself, and Tulindberg had him join in a performance of a subsequently lost Clarinet Quartet that represents the first known use of the ancient *runo* tune in classical music.

Acerbi's tale demonstrates that *runo* singing in the *Kalevala* tradition was commonly known and highly regarded in late 18th-century Finland. Tulindberg was the most significant composer of the Classical period in the land, and his pride in the *runo* tune reflected his awareness of the unique nature of this national tradition. Tulindberg's son Otto was involved in a project to create a *Singspiel* about Väinämöinen in the 1820s, but this project for some reason was never realized.

Acerbi, who listened to the music of the North from the perspective of a nation of opera, was not very sanguine about the future of Finnish music, as far as *runo* tunes were concerned: "Finns undoubtedly have a sensitive affinity for music and poetry. It would seem natural for these two art forms to proceed hand in hand, yet Finns are not as advanced in music as they are in poetry, due to the limitations of their national instrument and the love and respect which they hold for it and which prevents them from giving it up."

3 A myth is born:
Lönnrot's Kalevala and the first Kalevala compositions

The emergence of nation-states and National Romanticism in the early 19th century created a new demand for the cultural revisiting of ancient mythology. Herder's collection of folk poetry from all around Europe (*Stimmen der Völker in Liedern*, 1778–1791) equated national identity — and thereby the concept of the nation-state — with the individual folklore of a nation.

Among the Romantic philosophers, Schelling elevated art and artists into the highest manifestation of the divine, while Hegel outlined a model of history and a political theory which were taken up and developed in Finland by **Johan Vilhelm Snellman** (1806–1881), a statesman who supported the collecting and publishing of the *Kalevala* material. The role of the *Kalevala* in the forging of the nation-state had already been foretold in the general European ideological trend of the time.

The two roles of the Kalevala: the national and the international

Finland became an autonomous Grand Duchy in the Russian Empire with Sweden's defeat in the Russo-Swedish War of 1809. The music and folk poetry efforts that had emerged in Turku during the Enlightenment period withered when the capital was moved to Helsinki. Musical creativity flagged, and a large portion of the material that had been collected, including Porthan's folk poetry collections, was destroyed in the Great Fire of Turku in 1827.

Elias Lönnrot (1802–1884) published the *Kalevala* in the 1835 and again in its present form in 1849 (the 'New Kalevala'), but it was years before this new product was taken up in music. The explanation usually offered for this is that Finnish music in general was extremely undeveloped at the time and that there was no high-culture infrastructure in place.

There were no regular concert series, professional orchestras or public music education in Finland in the mid-19th century. Finnish-language literature was in its infancy, and in the early half of the century Finland was a politically and economically stagnant place.

The compilation of the *Kalevala* by Lönnrot and the national movement which it helped fuel did not become possible until an awareness of the necessity of having a culture of our very own penetrated the Finnish intelligentsia. The rise of the *Kalevala*, of Finnish music and of other art forms finally came together in the saga of national awakening that culminated in Finland's becoming independent in 1917.

The *Kalevala* acquired two separate roles in Finnish classical music, the national and the international. Artistic interpretations of the *Kalevala* were used as building blocks of the national identity and the nation-state, but its international representation necessarily required elements highlighting its exotic and culturally original nature on one hand and elements demonstrating its classical and aesthetically universal nature on the other. The latter involved drawing parallels between the *Kalevala* and other national epics and their respective functions.

The first steps of the Kalevala in classical music

Early attempts at using the *Kalevala* as a source of musical inspiration involved the wholesale importing of the subject matter into the conventional language of contemporary classical music. **Axel Gabriel Ingelius** (1822–1868) included a *Scherzo finnico* in his Symphony (1847), written in 5/4 metre as an allusion to runo singing. **Karl Collan** (1818–1871), a notable composer of solo songs, collected *runo* tunes and also translated the national epic into Swedish.

The *Kullervo Overture* (1860) by **Filip von Schantz** (1835–1865) was the first piece of music to make overt reference to Lönnrot's *Kalevala*. Its themes and symmetrical structure, complete with a recapitulation of the opening section, demonstrate a firm grounding in central European models.

Fredrik Pacius (1809–1891) wrote a historical opera entitled *Kung Karls jakt* (The Hunt of King Charles, 1852) to a libretto by Zachris Topelius, and inspired by its great popularity the two gentlemen began to outline a new work based on a story from the *Kalevala*. Pacius felt that their new project, *Princessan af Cypern* (The Princess of Cyprus, 1860), should be "Finnish through and through", although Topelius wished for something more "modern".

Princessan af Cypern is a fanciful transposition of the tale of Lemminkäinen to ancient Greece that we today might describe as postmodern. The work makes very little musical reference to the tradition of the *Kalevala*, but probably the greatest reason for later audiences finding the work alienating is that it displays the national mythology as an exotic and sometimes humorous curiosity. For audiences in the 1860s, the *Kalevala* was still only a primitive tale, a folk tradition whose values and beliefs were not quite appropriate as the foundation for works of art in the western style. Models for importing the *Kalevala* successfully into the realm of classical music had to be sought elsewhere.

Lemminkäinen, a womanizer and a tourist in Greece

Lemminkäinen and Kullervo have been the most popular *Kalevala* heroes among composers, Lemminkäinen perhaps ranking slightly above Kullervo nowadays. The difference between these two archetypally Finno-Ugric male protagonists is that Lemminkäinen is successful at everything in which Kullervo fails.

Lemminkäinen is ill suited to the traditional western Finnish image of what a man should be — stolid and dependable. He is a temperamental and impulsive womanizer and warrior, and he takes unnecessary risks. Lemminkäinen fits in smoothly into the gallery of musical Don Juan characters, and his questionable morals give composers leeway to use rather earthy musical means to depict him.

Jean Sibelius saw in Lemminkäinen a welcome antidote to the Finnish loser mentality: "I would like to see us Finns be a bit more proud, not always 'helmet askew'. What do we have to be ashamed of? This idea pervades *Lemminkäisen kotiinpaluu* (Lemminkäinen's Return). Lemminkäinen is a match for any count you might care to name. He is a nobleman, definitely a nobleman!" A similar nobleman's attitude to life and the opposite sex can be identified in Uuno Klami's adventuring Lemminkäinen, a "great scoundrel".

Aarre Merikanto wrote his *Lemminkäinen* as an orchestration study and as an opportunity for "speaking my mind about 'fiery imagination'". For the young composer, Lemminkäinen was a character to identify with, wooing Moscow girls with chocolates. In the abduction of Kyllikki, Merikanto depicted a "self-confident and bragging hero of a man", which strangely echoes the character of the Professor of Composition who scared female students witless in the 1950s.

In more modern works, Lemminkäinen has become something of a problem, and the disruptive asocial nature of the character has come to the fore. **Pentti Raitio's** Lemminkäinen is a gate-crasher at Pohjola, **Erik Bergman's** Lemminkäinen is an "arrogant and unpredictable adventurer", and Lemminki in **Aulis Sallinen's** *Rauta-aika* (The Iron Age) is an urban go-getter.

In the opera *Äidit ja tyttäret* (Mothers and Daughters) by **Tapio Tuomela**, masculine daydreams no longer appear. Instead, Lemminkäinen is a fish trapped in the net of his destiny, and — as Paavo Haavikko writes in the libretto — "women are the cauldron in which a man boils and ripens". There is something so threatening in the Lemminkäinen myth that the character has had to be brought under control, making it possible to show up his sexually inappropriate, anti-modern arrogance as an empty bubble.

The most joyful of all, however, is the first manifestation of Lemminkäinen in Finnish classical music in *Princessan af Cypern* (The Princess of Cyprus, 1860) by **Fredrik Pacius**. This work is based on the conceit that "the dream of Saari in the *Kalevala* is actually a Viking reminiscence from the Mediterranean" (Topelius). Lemminkäinen arrives on Cyprus, abducts Chryseis, daughter of Aphrodite, and sails with her back to Finland, where he conjures up a Greek temple complete with columns for his bride. But Chryseis (representing Kyllikki) pines for her homeland and eventually dies. This variant of Lemminkäinen has found a new incarnation with the emergence of mass tourism to the Greek islands.

4 Robert Kajanus tunes Lönnrot's kantele

"After bidding us welcome, he apologized to us, obviously abashed, that he was barefoot." Meeting Elias Lönnrot was abashing also for the then 17-year-old **Robert Kajanus** (1856–1933), who went to see the great man living in humble quarters in Sammatti in 1874.

Lönnrot could not read or write music, but he had notated *runo* tunes by numbering the strings of the kantele. Kajanus was requested to tune Lönnrot's kantele, a mundane task with lots of symbolic significance, and he later recalled the revelation he had had: "Being in his presence was restful for the soul, for the mental atmosphere around him was uncommonly pure."

In December of the same year, Kajanus wrote his first *Kalevala* composition, *Hymni*. In its text, written by Frans Tamminen, the missionary aspect of the national epic is already in full flow: "Kaiu Wäinön kansan kieli, kaiu vielä kunniaan! Woita wierahankin mieli, säveleitäs kuulemaan." ('Ring out, O language of Wäinö's people, ring out with glory! Win over the hearts of strangers too, that they might listen to your music.')

Kajanus studied in Leipzig and Paris in the 1870s. Wagner's operas naturally provided mythological inspiration. However, the idea for using folk tunes as the basis for classical music probably came from the Norwegian composers with whom Kajanus associated, Svendsen and Grieg.

This concept manifested itself in Kajanus's instrumental works as recasting folk melodies into major-minor tonality and tailoring them to the framework of central European Romanticism. Kajanus did not make use of *Kalevala*-type tunes in his instrumental works, and in his major vocal works he made use of contemporary poetry inspired by the *Kalevala* rather than the poetry of the epic itself.

This was the context in which he wrote two works entitled *Suomalainen rapsodia* (Finnish Rhapsody, 1881 and 1886) and *Kullervon surumarssi* (Kullervo's

Funeral March, 1880), which quotes a folk tune entitled *Velisurmaaja* (The Brother-Slayer). Kajanus took the themes used in these works mainly from printed literature. Here, Kajanus was still squeezing the folk tradition into an existing, foreign classical music environment into which some of the characteristic features of the national epic did not really fit.

A breakthrough in the *Kalevala* genre and in Kajanus's output came with *Aino*, written for the 50th anniversary of the national epic in 1885. The musical influences for this work came from Wagner, but the male voice choir section at the end demonstrates two important concepts: the *Kalevala* as a monument of Finnish culture, and the *Kalevala* culture as a symbol of the cultural and/or political tribulations of the Finns. "Soi, soi nyt kannel, mun murhe jo murtanee, soi, soi, se mun sydäntäni virvoittaa." ('Ring out, O kantele, I am broken by sorrow; ring out, it shall refresh my heart.' Anonymous text, probably by F. Tamminen.)

The kantele of Lönnrot was inherited by Sibelius, but we must not overlook the role of Kajanus in the *Kalevala* renaissance of Finnish music. It was he who bound the musical use of the *Kalevala* up with the Finnish nationalist movement, turned it into one of the cornerstones of Finnish high culture and used it as a weapon against the Swedish-speaking elite in the language war. It was also Kajanus who laid the groundwork for orchestral works inspired by the *Kalevala*.

5 Jean Sibelius discovers the tone of the Kalevala

Jean Sibelius (1865–1957) heard Kajanus's *Aino* while studying in Berlin in autumn 1890. Sibelius mentions that he had "grown fond of the *Kalevala* while still at school in Hämeenlinna", but hearing Kajanus's work may have been the final impulse for exploring the *Kalevala* musically.

Kajanus had had his *Kalevala* epiphany in Leipzig, and Sibelius had his while studying in Vienna. Later, Kuula wrote Kullervo songs in Bologna, Aarre Merikanto took Lemminkäinen off to war in Moscow, and Klami went to the library

of the Sorbonne to borrow a copy of the *Kalevala*. It was often the case that Finnish composers did not fully realize the potential of the national epic until they were abroad, far from the narrow confines of the national viewpoint. In foreign parts, the Finnish identity became clearer, and the original nature and exportability of the *Kalevala* became more obvious.

The Kullervo Symphony and trying to be Finnish

Declaring the *Kalevala* to be on a par with the great mythological poetry of the world did nothing to ease the pressure on artists. Like many other Finnish composers, Sibelius felt inadequate in the face of such a sacred task: "The more I explore the exploits of Kullervo, the smaller I feel myself and wonder whether I am audacious enough to imagine myself worthy of even attempting such a thing."

However, Sibelius immediately saw the *Kalevala* in terms of music, as is apparent from a letter he wrote to his fiancée Aino Järnefelt in Vienna in 1890; she had sent him a copy of the Kalevala. "I am busy reading the *Kalevala*, and I understand Finnish much better now. That one passage in the *Kalevala* (*Soitto on murehista tehty* [Music is made of sorrows]) is wonderful. I think the *Kalevala* is quite modern. It is all like music to me, a theme and variations. The action is always subordinate to the mood, the gods are men, Väinämöinen is a musician, etc."

Finnish culture in the late 19th century was torn by what was known as the 'language war', a struggle for hegemony between the traditional Swedish-speaking elite and the emerging Finnish-speaking intelligentsia. Sibelius, although a Swedish speaker by birth, attached himself at an early stage — not least because of his association with the Järnefelts — to the Fennomans, the Finnish nationalists and the 'Young Finnish' faction.

<<< Jean Sibelius (1865–1957) ESTABLISHED TWO DIFFERENT MUSICAL WAYS OF FRAMING THE FINNISH TRADITION IN CONCERT MUSIC: ALONGSIDE HIS MONUMENTAL SYMPHONIC MAJOR WORKS HE ALSO WROTE PIECES THAT ARE LIGHTER IN EXPRESSION AND INSTRUMENTATION. PHOTO: SIBELIUS MUSEUM.

The *Kalevala* culture became a prime weapon for 'Young Finnish' artists in the language war. Sibelius aligned himself with the cultural aspirations of the Young Finns and never advertised his concerts in the conservative, 'Old Finnish' newspapers, for instance. At the same time, however, he retained the cosmopolitan world view typical of the Swedish speakers, and this informed his view of the *Kalevala* as well.

In connection with the *Kullervo Symphony*, Sibelius emphasized the universal nature of his art as compared to the national: "Finnish, truly Finnish aspirations in music are something that I now understand less realistically yet more genuinely and truly than before. After all, one cannot be true in art just by knowing what it should be like; one must feel it."

Sibelius had heard the famous *runo* singer **Larin Paraske** (1833–1904) in Porvoo, and according to a bystander he had "jotted down tunes and rhythms". The composer later denied that he had had any knowledge of *runo* tunes when writing *Kullervo*. Sibelius rarely used direct quotes from folk songs or *runo* tunes in his work, and he also belittled the significance of these to his works, perhaps because he feared being branded a 'provincial composer' abroad.

In the *Kullervo Symphony* (1891), the 'genuine and true Finnish aspirations' did not translate into an idealization of the subject, but rather into an archaic-flavoured and musically radical approach, where the ancient nature of the *Kalevala* came across in a "quite modern" guise.

This approach also emerged in the competitions for illustrations for the *Kalevala* organized at about the same time. The depictions of Väinämöinen, Lemminkäinen and Kullervo submitted by artists surprised viewers and critics with their "ugliness". Sibelius's opening shot in the genre displays a similar austere and harsh flavour, like ancient Greek tragedy without the noble Hellenic figures.

Sibelius on the trail of runo tunes

After completing the *Kullervo Symphony*, Sibelius went on a poetry collecting trip to eastern Karelia in summer 1892. The first part of the trip, to Pielisjärvi, was his honeymoon with Aino, but Sibelius then went further east to Ilomantsi: "I heard the kantele being played by a woman who is considered weak in the head. She is said to have lost her reason after hearing the church bells of Valamo. Whatever the state of her wits, she was an excellent kantele player. — A great love took me over during that trip, and it remains strong with me."

In his test lecture in applying for the post of music teacher at the Imperial Alexander University in Helsinki in 1896, Sibelius (foreshadowing Bartók) proposed that folk tunes would play a role in dismantling conventional tonality, just as they had earlier played a role in consigning modality to history. "They had to yield to the tonality stemming from ancient folk songs. Now it is apparent that our present system of (major-minor) tonality is crumbling."

Delving into Sibelius's works in search of traces of *runo* tunes has not been politically correct in Finland, but folk song scholar A.O. Väisänen, who interviewed the composer on several occasions, found numerous occurrences, for instances in *Tuonelan joutsen* (Swan of Tuonela) and the melody of the *Ballad* in the *Karelia Suite*, in the opening movement of the First Symphony — the clarinet introduction and the alternating theme for two violins — in the second movement of the Second Symphony and in *Tapiola*. The influences are obvious in the second and third movements of the *Kullervo Symphony* as well as in *Lemminkäinen Tuonelassa* (Lemminkäinen in Tuonela) and in the Karelian trepak celebrating the hero's homecoming.

In some cases, *Kalevala* connections in Sibelius became a contentious issue. The Swedish-speaking factions rejoiced in the "ancient Ossian flavour" of *En Saga*, while the composer himself said to A.O. Väisänen: "It is entirely home-grown. How can anyone think of anything but Finland when listening to it?" Later, Sibelius explained to his private secretary Santeri Levas that *En Saga* was a deeply personal work: "In no other work of mine have I revealed myself as completely as in *En Saga*." The Kalevala origin of the themes in *En Saga* is in itself beyond question; one of them in fact appears in Lönnrot's notes.

Sibelius did use direct folk music quotes on occasions, for instance in the first tableau of the *Karelia* music (1893), where actual runo singers were brought on stage. The subject of the tableau — *Karjalainen koti vuonna 1293* (A Karelian home in 1293) and *Sodan sanoma* (Tidings of war) — was fired with a combative patriotic spirit. In the *Sanomalehdistön päivien musiikki* (Press Celebration Music, 1899; later *All'overtura in Historiallisia kuvia* [Historical Pictures], 1911), Väinämöinen delights nature and the people of *Kalevala* with his music. Sibelius intended to write a more ambitious piece on Väinämöinen's music-making, but the project never materialized.

What was more important than quotes or stylistic features was that the musical heritage of the *Kalevala* merged smoothly with Sibelius's personal and subjective musical idiom. The narrow compass of the themes gave scope to an original brand of symphonic motif processing. The endless repetition of *Kalevala* tunes sparked an ornamental variation technique where ornaments transformed into mythical ostinatos. Modality helped Sibelius distance himself from the major–minor tonality of western music.

From The Boat Journey to the Lemminkäinen legends

The trailblazer in the Finnish Kalevala music style turned out to be not the Kullervo Symphony (performances of which Sibelius later forbade) or the Lemminkäinen legends but Venematka (The Boat Journey), a partsong for male voice choir whose incisive Kalevala rhythm took Oskar Merikanto and the rest of the younger composer generation by a storm.

Apart from choral works based on the Kalevala such as *Heitä, koski, kuohuminen* (Cease, O Cataract, Thy Foaming) and *Terve, kuu* (Hail, O Moon), Sibelius also wrote more subtle choral works based on poems from the *Kanteletar* such as *Saarella palaa* (Fire on the Island), *Sortunut ääni* (The Broken Voice), *Soitapas, soria likka* (Play a Tune, O Fairest Maiden) and *Min rastas raataa* (The Thrush's Toiling), and particularly *Rakastava* (The Lover, 1893), originally written for male voice choir. This work is particularly interesting as an example of how Sibelius took his *Kalevala* style in an abstract direction: it is best known today in an adaptation for strings and percussion completed in 1911–1912.

After *Kullervo*, Sibelius's most ambitious project in this genre was the opera *Veneen luominen* (Building of the Boat), with Väinämöinen as the main character. This project never progressed beyond its initial stages, but its material drifted into the Lemminkäinen legends completed in 1896, including what was to have been the overture to the opera, *Tuonelan joutsen* (Swan of Tuonela). In *Lemminkäinen*, Sibelius parted company with the deliberate archaisms of the *Kullervo Symphony*, although he was still hesitating between the symphonic and the programmatic approaches.

How the Kalevala was integrated into Sibelius's idiom

Moving into the 20th century, *Kalevala* works took back seat in Sibelius's work in favour of the symphonies. This had to do both with the composer's international aspirations and with a deeper integration of the *Kalevala* themes into his idiom. For Sibelius, the *Kalevala* ultimately became perhaps more an expression of a Pantheist world view and a Jungian mindscape than a Romantic monument redolent with national symbolism.

Sibelius had originally intended to give *Pohjolan tytär* (Pohjola's Daughter, 1906) the title *Väinämöinen*, but his publisher convinced him otherwise. Inspired by the eighth *Runo* in the *Kalevala*, *Pohjolan tytär* is the most high-flying of all of Sibelius's tone poems, and in it the *Kalevala* style is completely buried in a shamanistic avalanche of brief ostinato and hoquetus motifs where new themes emerge out of the scraps of earlier ones.

Luonnotar for soprano and orchestra (1913) aims at a similar suggestive effect, but with considerably more austere means. The text comes from the first Runo of the *Kalevala*, a creation myth. The filigree string patterns hark back to Sibelius's earlier *Kalevala* works, but in other respects the composer is sailing a completely different sea. The texture spans several registers, reflecting the emptiness of the universe through which the soprano solo soars like the Maiden of the Air or the teal in the story.

Luonnotar is related to *Tulen synty* (The Origin of Fire), completed in 1902 for the opening of the Finnish National Theatre. Written for baritone, male voice choir and orchestra, it is a sombrely coloured work with echoes going back to the *Kullervo Symphony*. It is the richest of Sibelius's *Kalevala*-based cantatas.

By comparison, *Laulu Lemminkäiselle* (Song to Lemminkäinen), written in 1896 to a poem by Yrjö Weijola, is hamstrung by the limitations of its text, and *Väinön virsi* (Väinö's Song), written for the Sortavala Song Festival in 1926 with a text from the 43rd *Runo* of the *Kalevala*, is not one of the composer's better efforts.

In his final orchestral work, the tone poem *Tapiola* (1926), Sibelius tied together the symphonic and tone-poem strands of his output, fusing the *Kalevala*–Finno-Ugric with the abstract-universal. *Tapiola* alone should have alerted Finnish composers to the possibilities offered by the *Kalevala* beyond mere musical illustrations.

Minor works and aborted projects

Sibelius not only made more use of the *Kalevala* than any other Finnish composer, he also did so with the widest range of ensembles, styles and genres. He did deny, though, that his suite of three lyrical piano pieces entitled *Kyllikki* op. 41

(1904) had anything to do with Kyllikki in the *Kalevala* (whom Lemminkäinen abducts as his bride but who proves too obstinate for him); however, the piano suite does match the mood of the story admirably.

Similarly, the piece named after a minor character in the *Kalevala*, Lemminkäinen's rugged comrade-in-arms *Tiera* (1898), is scored with wonderful appropriateness for brass septet and percussion. The *Kalevala* offered Sibelius both grand and mundane subjects, opportunities for both profound artistic exploration and light, flowing narrative.

When Sibelius completed *Tapiola* in 1926, he still had numerous irons hot in the forge that created the Sampo. As late as in 1921, he was publicizing his sketches for Väinämöinen's song: "It is such a musically delicate subject; it brings together all the arts. The sequence where Väinämöinen weeps is pure music and easy to create."

Sibelius can hardly have been discussing the rather modest cantata *Väinön virsi*, which touches upon the vast vistas of the 34th *Runo* of the Kalevala as nonchalantly as the first tableau of *Historiallisia kuvia* deals with the Finnish variant of Orpheus. We may only speculate whether this powerfully symbolic subject had anything to do with the Eighth Symphony, which never saw the light of day.

In an interview in 1921, Sibelius also said that he would compose the tale of the Sampo: "I shall yet write something on that. The fascinating thing about the Sampo is that we do not know what the Sampo is. The forging of the Sampo must be all in pianissimo... as if at a great distance. Everything must be symphonically conceived." But in the cultural climate of the 1920s, it was becoming increasingly difficult to take up the *Kalevala*.

Kalevala for the masses

The *Kalevala* is originally folk poetry, but even in Lönnrot's editing we can see a trend towards artistic 'refinement' of the tales. Lönnrot hoped that his *Kalevala* would inspire artists in various fields, particularly composers, to create artworks worthy of the realm of western culture.

Indeed, the *Kalevala* has inspired Finnish composers to achievements of high artistic merit, merging it with visions of national grandeur, all-embracing pantheism or abstract primeval emotions. The profane features of folk poetry have given way to noble and elevated sentiments. However, there is a long tradition of substantially more earthy visions of the *Kalevala* in Finnish music.

What is surprising is that **Jean Sibelius** (1865–1957) was the origin of both the high and the low approach to the *Kalevala* in music. In his *Karelia* music (1893) and the *Sanomalehdistön päivien musiikki* (Press Celebration Music, 1899), Sibelius catered to the impression held by the upper classes of the *Kalevala*, and these pieces were much better received than the *Kullervo Symphony* and the *Lemminkäinen* legends. The famous *runo* singer Larin Paraske made a cameo appearance at the first performance of the *Karelia* music. Sibelius continued the popularization of the *Kalevala* in several choral works, but he steered clear of the subject in his solo songs.

Oskar Merikanto (1869–1924) wrote his opera *Pohjan neiti* (Maiden of the North, 1899) specifically as a *Kalevala* folk opera. It has later, perhaps unfairly, been criticized as naïve. The opera was a competition entry and received first prize from a jury that remarked: "The music of the opera is above all simple and melodious."

A more rustic flavour was sought by **Uuno Klami** (1900–1960), who dispensed with upper-class sensibilities altogether. Folk art was also the source for *Kalevala* works written in Soviet Karelia since the 1930s, under the doctrines of Socialist Realism. **Helmer Sinisalo** (1920–1989?), who wrote a ballet entitled *Sampo*, has said that Karelian composers "were attracted above all by the ideological strength of the epic, the depth and fascination of its characterizations, its artistic originality and the steadfast aspiration of the people of Kalevala towards peace and a brighter future".

Soviet aesthetics also formed the context for Estonian *Kalevala* music for quite a long time, but soon the *Kalevala* and its Estonian counterpart *Kalevipoeg* became a source of Estonian originality under difficult conditions. The dynamic primitivism of **Veljo Tormis** (b. 1930) in particular has inspired a number of followers, some of them in Finland: the *Kalevala*-based choral works and larger-scale works of **Pekka Kostiainen** (b. 1944) showcase folkloristic melodies and incisive, repetitive rhythms.

Popular settings of the *Kalevala* follow conventional interpretations of the poems, but the performing ensembles are sometimes quite unusual, as in the *Sampo Symphony* written by **Asko Vilén** (b. 1947) for concert band. A particularly welcome innovation is the children's opera *Kiljusten Kalevala* (The Kiljunens' Kalevala, 1998) by **Ilkka Kuusisto** (b. 1933), which has been followed by the acclaimed opera *Koirien Kalevala* (The Dogs' Kalevala, 2003) by his son **Jaakko Kuusisto** (b. 1974).

At its most successful, popularized *Kalevala* art has proven its potential for scoring hits, as with *Vesi väsyy lumen alle* (Water Under Snow Is Weary, 1976), a choral work by **Harri Wessman** (b. 1949) based on a traditional Kalevala tune and a stylistically appropriate poem by Eha Lättemäe.

6 "Let Sibba handle that" — Sibelius's contemporaries and the Kalevala

"There's nothing for you to do with the *Kalevala*, you let Sibba handle that and try to think of something else!" Thus pianist and composer **Selim Palmgren** (1878–1951) tried to convince himself at the beginning of the 20th century; he did not wholly stick to his promise, however.

Sibelius had forbidden performances of the *Kullervo Symphony* and two of the *Lemminkäinen* legends, thus giving space, at least temporarily, to other musical depictions of Kullervo and Lemminkäinen. Still, the shadow of Sibelius was felt perhaps more keenly in the matter of the *Kalevala* than in any other genres of music. Up to the 1920s Sibelius could be said to have held a sort of unspoken ius primae noctis regarding music based on the *Kalevala*.

But even without Sibelius, the *Kalevala* was quickly becoming an insurmountable obstacle for nationally-minded composers. **Toivo Kuula** (1883–1918) expressed his performance anxiety in writing: "I feel that *Kalevala* subjects, being so wonderful in themselves, require long and demanding work that must be refined in numerous fires before one can let it go out into the world." Kuula toyed with the idea of writing a Lemminkäinen piece for a long time but eventually wrote nothing: "It began to seem like a sacrilegious notion."

The topic of Lemminkäinen was addressed with rather conventional means by composers such as Ilmari Krohn, Väinö Haapalainen and Lauri Ikonen, but most composer shied away from this concept, whose arduous nature was hammered home by experts at every turn: "This sort of creative task, completely free and calling for almost boundless imagination and a largeness of mental capacity, is such a responsible and delicate endeavour that one can only consider it natural, even commendable, that only the very best composers have dared touch upon the subject." (Axel Törnudd, 1909)

Erkki Melartin, Aino and wild woodland theosophy

Leading composers strove to choose formats, styles and *Kalevala* stories with which they could avoid direct comparison with Sibelius. The opera *Aino* (1907) by **Erkki Melartin** (1875–1937) was a 'Kalevala mystery' where runo tunes were used as Leitmotifs; its theosophical symbolism and Wagnerian sound world supplanted Sibelius's mythological-suggestive world with a more fashionable brand of metaphysics.

Melartin's lyrical music imbues the tale of Aino with a civilized and peaceful aura. Väinämöinen appears as a wizard schooled by adversity who, in traditional Finnish fashion, learns to accept the facts and adapt to them. Melartin consciously sought out *Kalevala* subjects untouched by Sibelius in *Ilmarinen* (1908) and the incidental music for *Pohjolan häät* (Wedding at Pohjola, 1902, J.H. Erkko).

Melartin made his most original contribution to *Kalevala* music with his *Marjatta-legenda* (1914), the libretto for which came to him after Sibelius had discarded it. Melartin used Impressionist means and the feminine viewpoint which the subject encouraged to distance *Marjatta-legenda* from the sphere of blinkered National Romanticism. At the same time, the pale and modest lyrics of the libretto prevented the music from being too high-flying and universal.

Leevi Madetoja: The Kalevala through Ostrobothian eyes

For **Leevi Madetoja** (1887–1947), hearing Sibelius's *Venematka* was "like a bombshell", but his breakthrough work, the tone poem *Kullervo* (1913), has mostly been compared to Tchaikovsky's *Romeo and Juliet*. Although the influences are evident, *Kullervo* op. 15 is better than its reputation. Madetoja combines memorable themes and breezy orchestration in a compact form with a dexterity that is by no means self-evident in *Kalevala* compositions.

Madetoja was at his best *Kalevala*-wise in vocal works whose form and idiom had no obvious counterpart in the output of Sibelius. *Väinämöisen kylvö* (Väinämöinen's Sowing, 1919) for soprano or tenor soloist and orchestra differs from the mainstream of the genre in terms of its optimistic and constructive subject, but Madetoja's musical style was perhaps unduly cramped by the fact that the work was commissioned for the founding festivities of the Kalevala Society.

In his "symphonic portrait" *Sammon ryöstö* (The Stealing of the Sampo, 1915), Madetoja insightfully uses a major-key variant of a runo tune and manages to treat the dramatic and action-packed narrative without sombre pathos. The culmination of the work was, however, inspired by the dramatic fresco by Akseli Gallen-Kallela. What makes Madetoja's *Kalevala* compositions particularly interesting is his Ostrobothnian idiom, eschewing Karelianist clichés.

7 The Kalevala of the early Modernists

The National Romanticism of the Kalevala and Modernist trends were like chalk and cheese, and the cosmopolitan composer Ernest Pingoud never even touched the subject. Väinö Raitio too was ill at ease with this subject matter, but by contrast **Aarre Merikanto** (1893–1958) explored the topic of Lemminkäinen in three different works.

Written in Moscow, the *Lemminkäinen* tone poem (1916) was above all an orchestration exercise written for the class of Serge Vasilenko. Merikanto's *Lemminkäinen* may lack characteristic themes and structural integrity, but it does capture Lemminkäinen's breezy nonchalance and the cinematic progression of his tale.

Lemminkäinen is also the central character of the *Kyllikin ryöstö* (The Abduction of Kyllikki) dance music that Merikanto wrote for the centenary of the Kalevala. This work is characterized by lightly adapted folk dances, but the night scene *(Nocturne)* suddenly floods with the Modernist chromaticism of the

1920s, plunging the music into depths from which not even the furioso of the finale can extract it.

As an interesting anecdote, composer Usko Meriläinen, one of Merikanto's students, recalls that *Fantasia* (1923), one of Merikanto's major works, also has a Lemminkäinen connection. This is a fascinating concept, if for no other reason that the work contains nothing remotely resembling a musical *Kalevala* style.

The opera *Kullervo* (1917) by Armas Launis (1885–1959), based on the eponymous play by Aleksis Kivi, was the first application in Finland of folk music collection and research in the manner of Béla Bartók. Apart from *runo* tunes, Launis also collected *yoik* tunes of the Sámi and, later, Bedouin tunes.

8 The dream of Greater Finland: Growth of the national Kalevala cult

By the 1930s, National Romantic *Kalevala* music had reached the end of the road, but traditionalists would not accept any stylistic reforms.

Merikanto's folkloristic *Kyllikin ryöstö* is not one of his Modernist works, yet Selim Palmgren in a review shied away from any deviations of the traditional approach set in stone at the end of the 19th century: "Aarre Merikanto seems besotted by Stravinsky, a less than happy influence to apply at least in the case of Kyllikki, Lemminkäinen *et consortes.*"

Younger composers such as Uuno Klami began to look askance at the national epic: "Writing music to *Kalevala* subjects is not really a current topic in Finland today, not in any extensive way at least... I believe that if it comes around again, it will happen under different stars and different ideals."

On the other hand, ever since Finland's independence *Kalevala* art had begun to acquire a new set of pressures from the extreme right-wing movements dreaming of a Greater Finland and from the Academic Karelia Society.

Armas Launis and the birch-bark horn of Kullervo

"Leaning against a rock, he blew on his horn all alone in the wilderness, his thoughts evidently greyer than grey. He was not much to look at to begin with, and as his cheeks bulged and his eyes wandered when he struggled to produce a sound from his heavy-winded birch-bark horn, he looked quite horrible... How could I imagine that such an instrument could produce such melodies and such agile runs, or soaring, lyrical melodies?"

Armas Launis (1885–1959) ran into a genuine herdsman musician on a collecting trip in Ingria at the age of 19, and he wrote this reminiscence of the encounter for the annual of the Kalevala Society in 1920. Launis's field work produced the first Finnish sound recordings of folk tunes in the *Kalevala* tradition. Launis published the results of his collecting in 1910, but he also made use of this material in his opera *Kullervo*, completed in 1917.

Ingrian herders' tunes play a significant though not dominant role in the opera: the offstage bassoon solo that opens the work is one of two dozen Leitmotifs; it reappears for instance in the symphonic intermezzo in the final act. Cattle calls can also be heard in the English horn theme for Kimmo, Kullervo's childhood friend. The lullaby and lament sung by Kullervo's mother, the magic incantation of Ajatar (Mother Time) and the boisterous dance songs of the drunken Nyyrikki are also based on folk tunes. The Ingrian herdsman whom Launis met evidently also knew dance tunes: "Whether it be true or fancy, I felt that the horned cattle were fairly dancing to this music."

The themes collected by Launis travelled far for the performances of *Kullervo* in French in Nice and Monte Carlo in the 1930s and 1940s. One is reminded of the performance exhortation which the composer recorded in Ingria in 1903: "Don't just bawl along, listen too!"

Now, suddenly, "the essence of *Kalevala* poetry was quite simply the poetry of war" (Martti Haavio), and "now the *Kalevala* too rings with the noise of warlike mariners and shines with the glint of golden swords and the dragon-bedecked prows of warships" (Kaarle Krohn). The liberation of the '*Kalevala* tribes' of Karelia became the cornerstone of the new expansionist policy.

Conservative musical circles joined in. "We will rise someday; the memory of the wonderful, lofty *Kalevala* seems to assure us of it," wrote composer Heikki Klemetti. His leader in the music periodical Suomen Musiikkilehti in the national epic's centenary year of 1935 gives some indication of why Finnish composers seemed to dry up when faced with the *Kalevala*:

"Are we worshipful enough? No. Too frequently we allow our worship to stop at a fruitless silent remembrance. We do not allow the worshiped content to enflame our minds to take action in order to improve and elevate all things Finnish under these new circumstances."

It must be said to the credit of Finnish composers that very few went along with the military-heroic interpretation of the *Kalevala* which took over literature and fine arts; a possible exception is *Kullervon sotaanlähtö* (Kullervo Goes Off to War, 1942) by **Tauno Pylkkänen** (1918–1980), inspired by Akseli Gallen-Kallela's eponymous fresco.

By contrast, it is indicative how many composers failed dismally in writing commissioned works for major events in the centenary year of the *Kalevala*, most importantly that held along what was then the eastern border of Finland, in Sortavala in 1935.

Väinö Raitio's (1891–1945) *Lemminkäisen äiti* (Lemminkäinen's Mother, 1934) is an ill-begotten thing in comparison with his works of the 1920s. *Neiet niemien nenissä* (Maidens on the Headlands, 1935), which quotes a tune called *Valamon kirkonkellot* (Church Bells of Valamo), was more successful within the confines of its restricted style. Madetoja's cantata *Väinämöisen soitto* (Väinämöinen's Music-Making) is undoubtedly his least successful *Kalevala* work, and

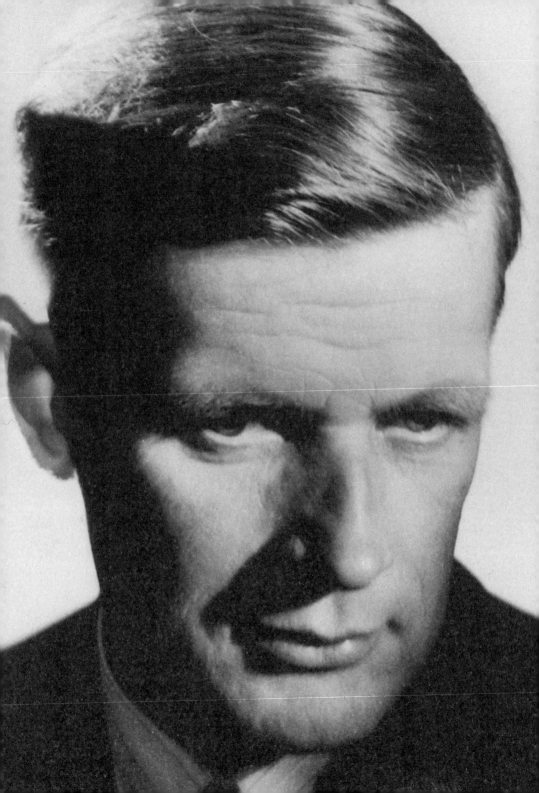

Sulho Ranta's (1901–1960) attempt at replacing the modern style with the popular in his *Väinämöisen laulu* (Väinämöinen's Song) was equally unconvincing.

9 Uuno Klami revisits ancient fields of honour

The most successful *Kalevala* work of the 1930s came from beyond the official pale, from a composer who had declared the entire genre suspect. **Uuno Klami** (1900–1961), like so many others, only got to know the national epic properly while studying abroad, in Paris, far from the jingoism of Finnish domestic politics.

Born in Virolahti, Klami had first touched upon eastern influences with his popular *Karjalainen rapsodia* (Karelian Rhapsody, 1927), whose raucous yet elegant style banished all Romantic pomp from musical depiction of common people. The *Tšeremissiläinen fantasia* (Cheremis Fantasy, 1931) combined a surprising orchestral Impressionism with its exotic and shamanistic subject.

Klami may have been toying with the idea of a *Kalevala* piece even before Robert Kajanus approached him, promising him that "it would be highly advantageous to the popularity of modern music for it to score a victory on the ancient fields of honour". Klami followed up on this nod from the National Romantic generation, but the long gestation of his *Kalevala Suite* (1932–1943) shows that renovating the musical image of the *Kalevala* was anything but easy.

A forerunner of the suite emerged in 1934 in the form of the scherzo *Lemminkäisen seikkailut saaressa* (Lemminkäinen's Adventures on the Island), where Sibelian eroticism had been replaced by a pulsating Stravinskian vitality. In the final *Kalevala Suite*, the function of this movement was taken by the more sensual *Terhenniemi*, which makes clever use of the archaic repetitiveness.

<<< Uuno Klami (1900–1960) WAS AT FIRST AVERSE TO THE IDEA OF WRITING MUSIC BASED ON THE KALEVALA. HOWEVER, OVER A LONG GESTATION PERIOD HE WROTE THE *Kalevala Suite*, WHICH IS A MILESTONE IN ITS GENRE AND A SIGNIFICANT STEP AWAY FROM THE NATIONAL ROMANTIC MUSICAL IMAGE OF THE NATIONAL EPIC. PHOTO: FIMIC.

The pressures experienced by the composer made the *Kalevala Suite* a heterogeneous entity. There are personal and original strokes in the work, but also belligerent swells and distilled simplicity — symptoms perhaps of the composer attempting to respond to the demands of the times. At some point, he seems to have conceived the suite as a choreographic work, as demonstrated by the evolutionary nature of its images: cosmogony, agriculture, Lemminkäinen episodes and finally people forging a new happiness for themselves.

The primeval *Maan synty* (Origin of the Earth) with its militant snare-drum part has been compared to Stravinsky's *Rite of Spring*, but this cosmic vision dissolves smoothly into the gentle pastoral *Kevään oras* (Shoots of Spring). *Terhenniemi* is the most balanced of the movements, a scherzo plumbing the feverish mood of a summer night. *Lemminkäisen kehtolaulu* (Lemminkäinen's Lullaby) features an elegiac melody that just falls short of functioning as a proper slow movement. *Sammon taonta* (Forging the Sampo) is a piece of metallic hammering that comes across as a populist finale.

Before the Second World War, Klami wrote the archaistic, chant-like *Vipusessa käynti* (In the Belly of Vipunen, 1938) for baritone, male voice choir and orchestra. This was an interesting experiment in discovering the magic atmosphere of *runo* chanting without using actual *runo* tunes or a primitive pulsating ostinato. *Vipusessa käynti* won a composition competition organized by the Laulu-Miehet male voice choir; second prize was awarded to the "defiant" *Ukri* by Aarre Merikanto, a setting of a mock-epic poem from the *Helkavirret* (Whitsongs) of Eino Leino.

Klami managed to transpose the musical image of the *Kalevala* into new spheres in the 1930s, but he failed — quite understandably given the circumstances — to transpose interpretations of the national epic into a new context. The dramaturgy of the *Kalevala Suite* demonstrates this: after a powerful and promising opening, the work ends up in a noisy culmination reeking of national monumentalism.

10 "The feelings of a peaceful state of mind". Kalevala music after the war

The end of the Second World War heralded a re-evaluation of the *Kalevala*, and as early as in 1947 music scholar A.O. Väisänen highlighted the pacifism of the national epic.

Now it was proclaimed that the weapons of Väinämöinen were spells and competitive singing, not the sword: "For example, the *Iliad*, the *Nibelungenlied* and the *Chanson de Roland* are all mainly about the tumult of battle. It is rare to find the inner voices of people in them, the feelings of a peaceful state of mind. Finnish ancient poetry, by contrast, is filled with melodious content, the enchantment of nature, the lustre of myth."

Finnish music too woke up to a new era and a new view of the *Kalevala*. "We really must shake off this stagnant, ever-repetitive National Romanticism," declared Sulho Ranta in lambasting *Väinämöisen karhunkaato* (Väinämöinen Slaying a Bear, 1949) written by Selim Palmgren for the centenary of the 'New Kalevala'.

New winds began to blow in the Finnish arts, and Modernism came to stay. The Modernists of the 1950s, unlike their predecessors in the 1920s, were internationally oriented, and the national manifesto of the *Kalevala* culture was seen as a hindrance to the universal aspirations of the new art.

Those composers that did continue working with the *Kalevala* did so under the national banner, mostly carried by inspiration from Romanticism or folklorist Naturalism. It was clearly understood that new interpretations of the national epic were needed, both in terms of content and in terms of musical settings, but good responses to these challenges were few and far between.

It was after the war that **Yrjö Kilpinen** (1892–1959) created his most massive solo song collection, the 64-song *Kanteletar cycle* op. 100 (1948–1950). The composer had been branded as a Nazi sympathizer, and perhaps because of this the *Kanteletar cycle* was ignored and forgotten. Nevertheless, the work was one of the most important new approaches to the matter of the ancient tradition, and its format and lyrical idiom bring it very close to the mood of original *runo* singing.

Aarre Merikanto had tried to go beyond the text of the *Kalevala*, to the Ur-Finnish subconscious, in his ten *Ugrian folk tunes* (1938), and in his final works around this theme he took up the mock-Kalevala poems in the *Helkavirret* (Whitsongs) of Eino Leino. *Ihalempi* (1953) was commissioned by the Laulu-Miehet male voice choir, and it was required to contain "preferably light and beauty, not power and defiance as in *Ukri*".

Uuno Klami had managed a spectacular feat of trailblazing in the 1930s, but after the war he was in serious difficulties with *Kalevala* topics. *Purren valitus* (The Boat's Lament), which is entered in his catalogue of works, has never been found, and his plans for an opera entitled Väinämöinen never got beyond the libretto stage. His most extensive project was the full-length ballet *Pyörteitä* (Whirls), a retelling of the Sampo myth to a libretto by set and costume designer Regina Backberg written in 1944.

Klami had called an early version of his *Kalevala Suite* 'Choreographical images from the Kalevala', and a dance work was entirely in tune with his French-oriented aesthetics. Due to a series of setbacks, *Pyörteitä* was never finished; it is now, however, possible to gain an overall impression of the work in the version completed by Kalevi Aho.

In *Pyörteitä*, Klami adopted a tighter, more emphatically rhythmic idiom, with the influence of Stravinsky and Prokofiev very much apparent. The orchestration, as far as we can tell from the surviving sections, is more austere than before. The description of the genesis of the Sampo in the 10th *Runo* of the *Kalevala* is very much symbolic due to the choreographic nature of the work, almost abstract, and it is curious that the genesis of this wondrous contraption is never even mentioned in the libretto outline.

Ahti Sonninen's tradition collage

Ahti Sonninen (1914–1984) became the figurehead of the young Modernism for a moment with his *Sinfonisia tuokioita* (Symphonic Moments, 1947), but in his Kalevala works he aimed at a simpler style. The song cycle *Lyökäämme käsi kätehen* (Let Us Join Our Hands Together, 1949) is dominated by traditional *runo* tunes and 5/4 meter, albeit treated in a novel way.

Taivahan takoja (Forger of Heaven, 1957) is also based on runo tunes and folk tunes, but Sonninen stripped them of all sentimentality and harmonizations related thereto. In the many *Kalevala* works he wrote in the 1960s (*Lemminkäisen äiti* [Lemminkäinen's Mother], *Iso tammi* [The Big Oak], *Kultaneidon taonta* [Forging the Gold Maiden], *Kyllikin ryöstö* [The Abduction of Kyllikki], *Sammon taonta* [Forging the Sampo], *Tulen synty* [The Origin of Fire], *Karhunpeijaiset* [Bear Wake]), Sonninen sought something approaching the original performance context by combining singing, chanting and movement.

Sonninen compiled all his ideas about the *Kalevala* and Finnish identity into *Suomalainen messiadi* (Finnish Messiad, 1958–1972). Here, the folk poems collected by Martti Haavio reflect one of the great conflicts of Finnish history, the clash between the pagan culture of the *Kalevala* and early Christianity, a clash in which thanks to the efforts of people like Mikael Agricola the Church gained the upper hand.

Suomalainen messiadi is an extensive, profuse and stylistically rich work which is difficult to pin down and which perhaps for this reason is little performed. In its aim to explore different sides of the Finnish character, different historical layers and different musical techniques from primitivism to dodecaphony, it ends up being more collage than credo. At the same time, it is an interesting forerunner to the national consensus and new unity of the 1970s.

Kokko by Tauno Marttinen and a new take on the Kalevala

The clearest break with tradition as regards setting the national epic to music after the war was made by **Tauno Marttinen** (b. 1912), whose work *Kokko, ilman lintu* (Kokko, Great Bird) triumphed over works by Merikanto and Klami in a composition competition in 1956. Marttinen had made his début as a composer with a number of late Romantic works in the 1930s; later, he expunged those works from his catalogue.

The primus motor behind Kokko was Marttinen's discovery of the *Kalevala*, and with this he was reborn as the 'Shaman of Hämeenlinna'. Initially conceiving the piece as a vocal work with no text, the composer could make no headway until he had taken up the *Kalevala*: "On the page where I opened it there was a poem about Kokko, the great bird. I left the opening as a vocalise. Then I discovered to my amazement that the *Kalevala* text was almost a perfect match to the vocal line I had already written. I underwent quite an internal upheaval... Then I plucked up courage and kept writing as far as I could. I only used the very basics of 12-tone technique. The main thing was that I had found a mental foundation."

The *Kalevala* became a source of immediate inspiration for Marttinen, a wellspring of vision-like primeval experiences. Marttinen too has sought to penetrate beyond Lönnrot's *Kalevala*, to earlier strata of folk poetry. His experience of the national epic is intuitive and linked to an irrationalist ideal of creativity following the spontaneous performance of a *runo* singer in a trance. Marttinen has written an exceptionally large number of *Kalevala* works, almost 25 pieces from solo works to extensive orchestral works. Marttinen has recorded his *Kalevala* faith in the book *Tuntematon Kalevala* (The Unknown Kalevala), where he explores links between the ancient Finnish faith and the great religions of the Orient, Hinduism and Buddhism. In this light, the *Kalevala* has turned into a mystic world force, a strand of a great synchretistic religion and a medium for primeval pantheistic experiences. Melartin's theosophical and pantheistic views on the *Kalevala* followed the same lines.

Tauno Marttinen (B. 1912) HAS WRITTEN NEARLY 25 WORKS BASED ON THE WORLD OF THE *Kalevala* OVER HIS EXTENSIVE CAREER. THE SHAMANIST LAYERS OF THE *Kalevala* AND THE ANCIENT TRADITION HAVE BEEN MORE IMPORTANT MUSICALLY, AESTHETICALLY AND IN TERMS OF LIFE PHILOSOPHY FOR MARTTINEN THAN FOR ANY OTHER POST-WAR COMPOSER. PHOTO: MANU MARTTINEN / FIMIC.

11 Kalevala music and the new national feeling

The musical image of the *Kalevala* was slow to change in the post-war period compared with how rapidly things were moving in music otherwise. We will also do well to remember how many composers did *not* touch the *Kalevala*: there is very little related to the national epic in the output of Paavo Heininen or Usko Meriläinen, or indeed of Erik Bergman before the 1980s.

This was also the case with the rise of the new wave of Modernism in the 1980s: looking for *Kalevala* topics in the catalogues of Magnus Lindberg, Kaija Saariaho, Jouni Kaipainen, Kimmo Hakola or Esa-Pekka Salonen is an exercise in futility. This aloofness has contributed to a limited viewpoint on the *Kalevala* in Finnish music throughout the end of the 20th century.

The 1960s, described as a radical period, was all but empty of *Kalevala* compositions. The 1970s in Finland have been described as a period of consensus where a concerted effort was made to marshal the nation's resources behind the common good and a shared outlook. The *Kalevala* became an object of interest for composers again in the 1970s, reflecting a revival of national themes and a relatively traditional musical idiom.

Pehr Henrik Nordgren: Biodynamic music to counterbalance technology

For example, the *Kalevala* works of **Pehr Henrik Nordgren** (b. 1944) can be seen as a reaction against modern society, both technocracy in music and the increasingly technical nature of the world in general. Nordgren uses various folk instruments and exotic composition styles to create a "non-digital" sound world that he has also described as "naturophony".

However, it is equally important that Nordgren's *Kalevala* works are separated from the sort of art that upholds patriotism, national monuments and heroic myths. In his *Kalevala* fantasy *Taivaanvalot* (The Lights of Heaven, 1985), Nordgren gives centre stage not to the heroes but to the swallow that brings light into the world. In the text too, Nordgren delves beyond Lönnrot's *Kalevala* to find older, pagan, original and therefore more universally human strata of poetry.

Taivaanvalot preserves the mythic primeval experience also by avoiding undue artistic polish: "I have consciously kept all original features as they are — including the occasional poor scansion of the poetry." In Nordgren's vision, the world of the *Kalevala* is not a nostalgic dream but a sort of survival guide. This is also reflected by the folk lament elements in his Fourth and Fifth Symphonies, which go back to the viola duet in the finale of *Taivaanvalot*.

Nordgren has also approached the *Kalevala* in certain choral works (*Maan alistaminen* [Subjugating the Earth], 1973; *Väinämöisen rukous* [Väinämöinen's Prayer], 1984; *Iso tammi* [The Great Oak]), but after *Taivaanvalot* he did not touch on the genre again until the dramatic ballad *Tuuri* (2003), a setting of a poem from the *Helkavirsiä* (Whitsongs) of Eino Leino. The universal message of the inevitability of death is partly associated with Lemminkäinen's going berserk at the party in Pohjola: "Never may gods feast with mortal men! Gods have long feasts, men's lives are brief, passing rapidly like a wheel turns."

The un-Kalevala adventurers of Rauta-aika

In retrospect, we may claim that the operas written by **Aulis Sallinen** (b. 1935) in the 1970s point directly towards the *Kalevala*. This cannot have been as obvious to the composer at the time, although the opening of *Ratsumies* (The Horseman, 1975) and the folk lament motif in *Punainen viiva* (The Red Line, 1978) — a vignette very much like the kantele player in Pacius's opera *Kaarle-kuninkaan metsästys* (The Hunt of King Charles) — foreshadowed what was to come.

Rauta-aika (The Iron Age, 1983), a television series on which Sallinen collaborated with author **Paavo Haavikko** (b. 1931) and director **Kalle Holmberg** (b. 1939), continued the analysis of power, greed and geography which Sallinen had already embarked on in his operas and whose critical content was aimed at the pragmatic foreign policy of the Finnish government under President Urho Kekkonen. The heroes of this series — Väinö, Ilmari and Lemminki — were deliberately un-*Kalevala* adventurers.

Rauta-aika and the orchestral suite which Sallinen adapted from the incidental music in 1985 provide a rare materialist viewpoint on the national epic: these heroes feed their own greed with dreams of the Sampo and end up as marauders invading a fictional Byzantium. One of the finest moments in the boisterous, adventurous score is the depressed *Väinön soitto* (Väinö's Music), a quiet expression of grief.

Sallinen's opera *Kullervo* (1988), based on the eponymous play by Aleksis Kivi, is a study of the insecurity of the Finnish psyche and the violence in which it finds an outlet. As in ancient Greek tragedy, all positive efforts turn against the protagonist; only his mother's love shines with a pale but lasting light.

Sallinen's *Kullervo* became a showpiece for Finnish music exports and for the sort of *Kalevala* exoticism tailored for foreign consumption when the opera received its world premiere in Los Angeles in 1992 and was later performed in Nantes, France. This was probably what caused Sallinen to focus on the universal and timeless nature of the title character rather than his Finnish features.

Einojuhani Rautavaara's Kalevala trilogy

The title of chief architect — or head gardener — of the new musical approach to the *Kalevala* must go to **Einojuhani Rautavaara** (b. 1928), who particularly in his opera trilogy *Marjatta, matala neiti* (Marjatta, Lowly Maiden, 1975), *Sammon ryöstö* (The Tale of the Sampo, 1982) and *Thomas* (1985) cast the mythology in an innovative musical guise.

In *Marjatta*, the tension comes naturally from the geopolitical setting and the juxtaposition of pagan and Christian culture. The performing ensemble — children's choir, percussion, flute and narrator — lends the work the lucidity of a legend.

Sammon ryöstö, by contrast, is set in a wholly manly world, amusingly flavoured by a synthesizer recalling the disco sounds of the 1970s. The magic milling machine, presaging the rise of the IT business, is carried by Finnish Vikings, *Kalevala* heroes out to build a nation, who in the end lose the key to a better future but sow the seeds of dreams in its place.

Thomas, written for the 150th anniversary of the *Kalevala* celebrated at the Joensuu Song Festival, is the most extensive and many-layered of the three works. Here, the *Kalevala* is principally just an environment into which the English-born Bishop Thomas is cast to become the spiritual leader of the Finns in the early 13th century. The Catholic invasion threatens the ancient rituals, which here too are linked by synchretistic association to eastern religions, for instance to the *Rigveda*. The setting and style are somewhat reminiscent of Karol Szymanowski's opera *King Roger*.

Thomas is, for all its stylistic plurality, a coherent entity whose suggestive music helps the listener look at the *Kalevala* with a much broader mind, penetrating through and past the text into the Finnish subconscious.

Rautavaara's view of the *Kalevala* is part of a national introspection specifically aimed at us Finns: "The *Kalevala* is the thread which, held in our hand, allows us to feel the vibrations that in the whole world, in all nations, in all cultures have started from the same point from which this thread is coming."

Apart from his opera trilogy, Rautavaara has written instrumental works featuring a fresh look at the heritage of the *Kalevala*, such as *Suomalainen myytti* (Finnish Myth, 1977) for strings and *Ugrilainen dialogi* (Ugrian Dialogue, 1973) for violin and cello.

Rautavaara's *Kalevala*-based choral works are miniatures that include use of irony, rare in the Finnish context, such as ritual mocking of the bride (*Morsian* [The Bride], 1975) or send-ups of how Finns behave when drunk or of Finnish laments (*Serenadi oluelle* [Serenade to Beer] and *Serenadien serenadi* [Serenade of Serenades], 1978), as well as a self-portrait defending an individual voice (*Laulaja* [The singer], 1956).

12 New avenues from the 150th anniversary

Finnish *Kalevala* music was for a long time characterized by a stylistic, functional and ethnic homogeneity; the field has been subject to renovation from time to time, but it was not until the 1980s that it splintered into clearly differing viewpoints.

Interpretations of the *Kalevala* no longer necessarily focus on the destiny of the nation, the identity of the Finnish majority or its aesthetics. However, even in the 150th anniversary festivities of the *Kalevala* in 1985 it was the national perspective that came foremost, even though the works commissioned for the anniversary were specifically intended to go against official policies or stylistic recommendations. Composers were apparently still getting their challenges from somewhere on high.

Ever since the days of the language war, Swedish-speaking composers had usually gone out of their way to avoid the *Kalevala*, but in the commissions for the 1985 anniversary, a bridge was built in this direction. **Einar Englund** (1916–1999) imbued his *Kanteletar Suite* (1984), his only *Kalevala* composition, with a profound Neo-Classicism.

Erik Bergman (b. 1911) had been through Scandinavian and Oriental mythology in his works before grappling with *Lemminkäinen* (1985), which was completely different from its counterpart in its composer's use of a freely written choral technique devoid of 'Ugrisms'.

In Bergman's case, one commission led to another: *Careliana* op. 112 (1988), written for the King's Singers to perform at the Joensuu Song Festival, combines cattle calls with bass ostinato shamanism and variations on runo songs, yet concludes the proceedings with raucous laughter. In *Lament and Incantation* (1986), Bergman also uses East Karelian *runo* tunes.

The *Kalevala* anniversary commission inspired Bergman to write a number of *Kalevala* works in which the national mythology is set in the context of universal mythology. *Loitsut* op. 105 (Incantations, 1989) for male voice choir delve into the power of words by exploring the very core of sound and gesture.

In the choral work *Tapiola* (1991), Bergman uses the familiar 5/4 metre but also presents a humorous portrait of the Tapiola suburb in Espoo. No wonder, then, that *Väinämöinen* op. 147 (2000) is a bit of a self-portrait of the nonagenarian composer — not least because here the text is from a Swedish translation of the *Kalevala*.

Modernist composers were also invited to participate in the 150th anniversary of the *Kalevala*. **Olli Kortekangas** (b. 1955) voiced his doubts (Finnish Music Quarterly 1985): "The Finns' conception of a genuine and natural *Kalevala* aesthetic is still a strange combination of composer-centred thinking dating from the Romantic era, a sort of 'back to the wilderness' nostalgia and national pride nurtured by a well-developed inferiority complex."

Kortekangas responded to the anniversary commission by writing *MAA* (Earth, 1984–1985) for children's choir and percussion. Its text comes not only from the *Kalevala* but also from the Chinese *Book of Changes*, the Bible and the poems of Walt Whitman. *MAA* is an "open and rugged" work whose global conception of the visible and the invisible is conciliatory rather than declaratory.

One of the most innovative premieres of the anniversary year was *Soitto* (Music) by **Eero Hämeenniemi** (b. 1951), premiered in Stockholm. Kalevi Aho wrote in his book *Suomalainen musiikki ja Kalevala* (Finnish Music and the Kalevala, 1985) that despite the challenging and gratifying nature of the subject, the description of Väinämöinen's music-making in the 41st and 44th *Runos* of the *Kalevala* has generated largely uninspired musical settings, among which Hämeenniemi's work is a brilliant exception.

Hämeenniemi has turned the idea of the poem into an abstract poem and creates an impression of music that spreads from a tiny initial germ throughout the orchestra and begins to have a life of its own through variations. One cannot help but think that modern thinking has finally given wings to Väinämöinen's vision.

13 New pathways: Kalevala music today

Although the musical treatment of the *Kalevala* has diversified significantly in recent years, we should note that only few composers in the youngest generation, for instance, are interested in the subject.

The list of composers with only a nodding musical acquaintance with the national epic contains some surprises: Joonas Kokkonen wrote only one choral piece, to a commission, and **Kalevi Aho** (b. 1949), who has even written a book on Finnish music and the *Kalevala*, has mainly contributed to the genre with his *Symphonic Dances*, which grew out of his work in completing the ballet Pyörteitä, and as such represents a homage to Klami rather than to the *Kalevala*.

Austrian-born **Herman Rechberger** (b. 1947) and Ukrainian **Fridrich Bruk** (b. 1937) have explored the Finnish national mythology from their respective viewpoints. **Jarmo Sermilä** (b. 1939) made the connection between *Kalevala*-style repetition and modern-day minimalism in *Myyttinen mies* (Mythical Man, 1982) for percussion quintet and *Hiiet hirveä rakenti* (Ogres Built an Elk, 1984) for trombones, percussion and tape.

Modern composers have typically distanced the *Kalevala* from its ideological and textual origins. *Ecrit sur le vent et l'eau* (2000) by Olli Kortekangas contains the 'origin of words' section from the *Kalevala* in a Latin translation. *Galdr* for clarinet and horn by **Harri Vuori** (b. 1957) refers to the Kalevala through Germanic spell chants, and *Veno* (Boat, 2000) by **Lotta Wennäkoski** (b. 1970) refers to the national epic through the archaic spelling of its title.

Contributions to the body of *Kalevala* music have also been made towards the end of the 20th century by composers such as Pentti Raitio, Jouko and Jyrki Linjama, Tapani Länsiö, Mikko Heiniö, Pekka Jalkanen, Tuomo Teirilä, Timo-Juhani Kyllönen, Heikki Valpola, Jaakko Mäntyjärvi and Harri Viitanen. Among these are choral music specialists Tapani Länsiö and **Jaakko Mäntyjärvi** (b. 1963), whose famous *Pseudo-Yoik* and *Kalevala*-based *Runo alotteleikse* (The Poem Beginneth, 1996) represent a new dimension in vocal music.

Jouko Linjama (b. 1934) has skirted around the *Kalevala* with poems by Runeberg (*Två sånger för manskör* [Two Songs for Male Voice Choir], 1974), texts by Lönnrot (*Vaeltaja-vaeltajalle* [Wanderer – To a Wanderer], 1999) and various lullabies (*Inkeriläiset liekkuvirret* [Ingrian Lullabies], 1984; *Unilintu* [Dream Bird], 1989), while the six-movement *Kalevala Suite* (1981) aims to mediate between the pagans and the Christians.

Pekka Jalkanen (b. 1945) has approached the *Kalevala* through its performers, in his music on the life of Larin Paraske (*Sijan tiiän kussa synnyin* [I Know the Place Where I Was Born], 1980) and in his music for traditional instruments, such as the Kantele Concerto (1997) and Kantele Septet (1987), which trace the instrument's history from ancient Greece. In his choral works, Jalkanen has focused on the *Kalevala* tradition in the oral tradition in particular, showing the matriarchal legacy of folklore in works such as *Vägehens otetut neidizet* (The Abduction, 1982), *Katrin parannus* (Katri's Salvation, 1984), Piika pikkarainen (The Little Lass, 1985) or the Christmas tale *Muaemo* (Earth-Mother, 1999).

Somewhere between primitivism and Neo-Classicism we can find the *Kalevala* choral songs of **Heikki Valpola** (b. 1946), many of them written for the Kullervo Choir which the composer conducts. *Tulenteko* (Fire-making, 1985) for accordion, piano and percussion is perhaps Valpola's best-known *Kalevala* composition dramatically illustrating ancient rites.

Tapio Tuomela and the women of the Kalevala

The young composer with the keenest interest in the *Kalevala* is **Tapio Tuomela** (b. 1958), whose principal work to date is the opera *Äidit ja tyttäret* (Mothers and Daughters, 1999), drawing on the tale of Lemminkäinen and written for the 150th anniversary of the 'New Kalevala'.

Many of Tuomela's *Kalevala* works (*Lemminkäinen* for orchestra; *Lemminkäisen monologi* [Lemminkäinen's Monologue]; *Lemmin loitsu* [Lemmi's Spell] for kanteles; *Tuli tuuli, tuli aalto* [Wind Came, Water Came; Lamentation] for soprano and ensemble; *Lamentation I–II*) are chips off this log, but there are also independent choral works (*Rondo* and *Rondino*) and vocal works (*Liekut ja Loitsut* [Images de Kantéletar]).

In *Äidit ja tyttäret*, Lemminkäinen, the grand womanizer of the Finno-Ugric tradition, the carefree adventurer and impulsive wanderer, has become a fish trapped in the net of fate. The title character derives a pagan sort of attraction from the love-magic poems that were originally censored from the Kalevala, but Paavo Haavikko's libretto leaves no room for masculine daydreams: it's the women who are running the show.

The subject required Tuomela to take a stand with regard to the *Kalevala* tradition, and he gave much thought to how to embed folk tradition in a Modernist idiom. The solution was one typical of our pluralist age: *Äidit ja tyttäret* features the 'new folk music' that emerged in the 1980s, while a *runo* tune recorded by Iivana Onoila over a century ago is employed in a Modernist Leitmotif technique.

Tuomela's opera focuses on a psychological power struggle and elements of the Kalevala that still form part of the mental makeup of all Finns. With its heterogeneous style and cleverly outlined subject, it demonstrates that the *Kalevala* still lends itself to a variety of musical styles and interpretations.

Tapio Tuomela (B. 1958) HAS REFASHIONED ELEMENTS FROM THE ANCIENT TRADI-
TION IN HIS WORK. HIS OPERA *Äidit ja tyttäret* (MOTHERS AND DAUGHTERS, 1999)
IS A NOVEL LOOK AT THE TALE OF LEMMINKÄINEN, WITH WOMEN AS THE DOMI-
NANT FORCE; ITS SCORE COMBINES THE LANGUAGE OF MODERNIST OPERA WITH
ETHNIC SINGING. PHOTO: MAARIT KYTÖHARJU / FIMIC.

Now, at the beginning of the 21st century, we may note that the range of Finnish *Kalevala* compositions has grown at a gratifying rate. However, very few of the youngest generation of composers are interested in the subject, as it is still considered to carry nationalist baggage and the stigma associated with it.

The *Kalevala* is cultural capital that belongs to all Finns, not just the powers that be and official Finland. Even critical commentary would be better than ignoring it altogether. On the other hand, it might not be such a bad idea to let the *Kalevala* rest for a while and accumulate spontaneous energy with which to inspire.

The sung Kalevala

The *Kalevala* is by its very nature sung epic folk poetry, but despite this solo songs and choral works based on it have received less attention than orchestral works. Even in discussions of *Kalevala* vocal music, the focus is on monumental works with orchestral accompaniment.

"Every composer knows the restrictions of the couplet metre of the *Kalevala*, which renders music too broad and prevents its passionate soaring," wrote Jalmari Finne, librettist of Erkki Melartin's opera *Aino* and his *Marjatta-legenda*, in 1909. Composer Tauno Marttinen has also observed that the metre of the *Kalevala* easily makes a composition too "boring and foursquare".

This was not a problem for those early composers who took up the *Kalevala* in a foreign language. A *Kalevala* opera in English planned in the 19th century by **Lafcadio Hearn** (1850–1904; known for his *Kwaidan* stories) and **Herman Krehbiel** (1838–1923) remained on the drawing board, but German conductor **Karl Müller-Berghaus** working in Turku completed his opera *Die Kalewainen in Pochjola* in German in 1890.

Müller-Berghaus conceived his opera as a set of highlights from the *Kalevala*, and its music "showed an undeniable Wagner influence, though with concessions to earlier brands of Romanticism" (Gils van der Pals). In his dedication, Müller-Berghaus dressed the content of the *Kalevala* in a Wagnerian guise: "Kalevalalle pyhitän tään työn, sen sankarlaulu laantumatta soi, min kaiku muinaisella mahdillaan, kuin koljon huuto toistaa ainiaan: Yö voittakaa! Vallatkoon valo maan!" ('To Kalevala I dedicate this sacred work, its heroic song shall never fade, like the echo of ancient might, like a giant's cry it repeats: Conquer the night! May light triumph over the earth!')

Jean Sibelius (1865–1957) hit upon a successful cadence for setting the rhythm of the Kalevala on his first attempt, in the *Kullervo Symphony*, fitting the text naturally into the whole. The repetitiveness of the poetry continued in the ostinato figures of the music, whose variation and development became an important part of Sibelius's motif processing. Sibelius himself often said that *runo* singing required continuous variation.

Oskar Merikanto (1869–1924) was not completely successful in fitting the *Kalevala* metre into Italian opera style in his *Pohjan neiti* (Maiden of the North). "Such errors of setting poetry would never be found in the products of older civilizations," Axel Törnudd chided him. The handling of text in the opera *Kullervo* by **Armas Launis** (1885–1959) was also panned as "peculiar speech-singing". Despite efforts by Melartin, Väinö Raitio (*Väinämöisen kosinta* [Väinämöinen's Wooing], 1937) and Aapo Similä (*Lemmin poika*

[Lempi's Son], 1960), *Kalevala* opera never really took off before the end of the 20th century. The opera *Sampo* (1945) written by **Leonid Vishkaryov** in Soviet Karelia has remained unknown in Finland.

Even in the early years of the 20th century, the standing recommendation was to write oratorios and cantatas rather than operas based on the national epic. A great number of such works was indeed written, but this genre never proved very innovative. Many of these works were written with the technical capacity of Finnish choirs in mind, and with musical expression limited by conventional conceptions of the *Kalevala*. Often, such works were performed at festivities on patriotic holidays.

The most prolific writer of *Kalevala* choral works was **Olavi Pesonen** (1909–1993), a student of Madetoja's. In his 40-odd choral songs, Pesonen purposely kept to a simple style so as to make the songs accessible to school choirs and youth choirs. His most extensive *Kalevala* work, *Ajat eellehen menevät* (Times Are Forward Going) is a relatively early work (1935).

Yrjö Kilpinen (1892–1959) wrote a few solo songs to poems from the *Kanteletar* in 1914–1915, but a collection and study trip to Ladoga Karelia in 1916 brought him into direct contact with runo singing.

Kilpinen never took an interest in *Kalevala* Romanticism or in folklorist simplification. Having taken up the *Kanteletar* again after the Second World War, he went straight for what Seppo Nummi described as "the mother lode of the folk *melos* of the Finno-Ugric peoples". The astounding *Kanteletar cycle*, with 64 songs, was given the symbolic opus number 100 by the composer.

For Kilpinen, who had mainly been working with Lieder in the German style, the *Kanteletar cycle* was an opening towards an 'eastern', impulsive, Mussorgskian mindscape. Most of the songs in the collection are narrow in compass and modal just like *runo* tunes, but being an experienced composer of solo songs, Kilpinen also gave scope for vocal brilliance and acerbic harmonization.

Most Finnish composers have written something for choir with a text from the *Kalevala*. Even **Joonas Kokkonen** (1921–1996), who never went near the tradition otherwise, wrote a piece for male voice choir entitled *Sormin soitti Väinämöinen* (Thus Played Väinämöinen's Fingers) to celebrate the unveiling of the restored painting by Robert Wilhelm Ekman entitled *Väinämöisen soitto* (Väinämöinen's Music), which had been damaged in a fire.

In more recent works, the problem of discrepancy between scansion and text rhythm has been solved in a variety of ways. **Pekka Kostiainen** (b. 1944), one of the most frequent setters of *Kalevala* texts in recent decades, has followed the natural cadence of the poetry in many of his choral works.

In *Tuli on tuima tie'ettävä* (Do Not Play With Fire, 1984), Kostiainen justifies his solution thus: "Since I ended up using a *Kalevala* text, I decided to use the style of runo singing in the music too, with constant repetitions and very narrow melodies with only three, four or five notes. These choices are intended to convey the primeval strength of this, our oldest and most genuine folk music, to people today."

Kostiainen's folkloristically oriented songs form a number of narrative cycles, such as *Marin tarina* (Mari's Tale, 1985) based on the chants of an Ingrian runo singers, *Sulhasen tulolaulut I–II* (The Bridegroom's Arrival Songs, 1988 and 1991), *Pakkasen luku* (The Frost's Incantation, 1983) or *Väinämöisen Tuonelanmatka* (Väinämöinen's Journey to Tuonela, 1989). The logical next step came with the *Kalevala* chamber operas *Joukahaisen runo* (Joukahainen's Poem, 1985) and *Sammon tarina* (The Tale of the Sampo, 2002). Kostiainen's interest in runo tunes also shows in his instrumental works (*Concerto non troppo*, 1982).

Select discography

BIS = BIS-CD | F = Finlandia Records | ODE = Ondine ODE

Aho, Kalevi
- *Pyörteitä* (Whirls, I act) (Klami–Aho). Lahti CO, Vänskä. BIS 696 (1997).
- *Symphonic Dances. Hommage à Uuno Klami*. Lahti CO, Vänskä. BIS 1336 (2004).

Bergman, Erik
- *Lament and Incantation* Op. 106. Tuomela, Fredriksson. ODE 774-2 (1991).

Englund, Einar
- *Kanteletar-sarja* (Kanteletar Suite). Serena Choir, Sikström.
Finngospel FGCD 1084 (1997).

Kajanus, Robert
- *Finnish Rhapsody no. 1* in D minor Op. 5; *Kullervo's Funeral March* Op. 3; *Aino*.
YL, Lahti SO, Vänskä. BIS 1223 (2004).

Klami, Uuno
- *Kalevala-sarja* (Kalevala Suite) Op. 23
1) Finnish RSO, Segerstam. F 4509-99968-2 (1987/1996). (+ Tsheremissiläinen fantasia)
2) Turku PO, Panula. Naxos 8.553757 F (1998). (+ Lemminkäisen seikkailut saaressa)
- *Karjalainen rapsodia* (Karelian Rhapsody) Op. 15. Finnish RSO, Oramo.
ODE 859-2 (1995). (+ Lemminkäisen seikkailut saaressa; Vipusessa käynti)
- *Lemminkäisen seikkailut saaressa* (Lemminkäinen Adventures on the Island of Saari)
1) Lahti SO, Vänskä. BIS 658 (1993–1994).
(+ Laulu Kuujärvestä; Suites No. 1 & 2 from the Ballet 'Whirls')
2) Finnish RSO, Oramo. ODE 859-2 (1995). (+ Karjalainen rapsodia; Vipusessa käynti)
3) Turku PO, Panula. Naxos 8.553757 F (1998). (+ Kalevala Suite)
- *Pyörteitä* (Whirls)
1) (I act; arr. by Aho) Lahti CO, Vänskä. BIS 696 (1997).
2) (Suites No. 1 & 2). Lahti CO, Vänskä. BIS 658 (1993–1994).
(+ Lemminkäisen seikkailut saaressa; Laulu Kuujärvestä)
- *Tšeremissiläinen fantasia* (Cheremis Fantasy) Op. 19. Noras, Helsinki PO, Panula.
F 4509-99968-2 (1973/1996). (+ Kalevala-sarja)
- *Vipusessa käynti* (In the Belly of Vipunen). Lindroos, The Polytech Male Choir,
Finnish RSO, Oramo. ODE 859-2 (1995). (+ Lemminkäisen seikkailut saaressa;
Karjalainen rapsodia)

Kokkonen, Joonas
- *Sormin soitti Väinämöinen* (Väinämöinen Plucked the Strings).
YL, Hyökki. F 0630-17694-2 (1997).

Kortekangas, Olli
- *MAA*. Tapiola Choir, Pohjola. F 1576-59921-2 (FACD 921) (1988).

Kostiainen, Pekka
- 'Kostiainen conducts Kostiainen 4: Poikako vai tyttö? (Boy or Girl?)'.
Marin tarina; Sulhasen tulolaulut I–II; *Pakkasen luku.* Musica Choir, Kostiainen.
Alba NCD 21 (2003).

Madetoja, Leevi
- *Kullervo* Op. 15. Finnish RSO, Saraste. F 4509-99967-2 (1996).

Melartin, Erkki
- *Aino*. Korhonen, Tiilikainen, Paasikivi, Dominante Choir, Lahti SO, Söderblom.
BIS 1193/94 (2002).

Merikanto, Aarre
- *Fantasia*. Finnish RSO, Segerstam. F 4509-99970-2 (1986/1996).
- *Lemminkäinen* Op. 10. Tampere PO, Ollila. ODE 905-2 (1998).

Pacius, Fredrik
- *Princessan af Cypern*. Åman, Storgård, Jubilate Choir, Tapiola Sinfonietta,
Söderblom. BIS 1340 (2004).

Raitio, Väinö
- *Neiet niemien nenissä* (Maidens of the headlands). Tapiola Sinfonietta, Ollila.
ODE 975-2 (2003).

Rautavaara, Einojuhani
- *Marjatta, matala neiti* (Marjatta, the Lowly Maiden). S. Rautavaara, Sippola,
E. Rautavaara, Tapiola Choir, Pohjola. F FACD 921 (1988).
- *Runo 42 'Sammon ryöstö'* (The Myth of Sampo). Nyman, Tiilikainen, Suhonen,
E. Rautavaara, YL, Hyökki. ODE 842-2 (1995).
- *Thomas*. Hynninen, Lindroos, S. Rautavaara, Savonlinna Opera Festival Chorus,
Joensuu CO, Haapasalo. ODE 704-2 (1988).

Sallinen, Aulis
- *Punainen viiva* (The Red Line) Op. 46. Hynninen, Valjakka,
Finnish National Opera C & O, Kamu. F 1576-51102-2 (FACD 102) (1979/1990).

- *Ratsumies* (The Horseman) Op. 32. Salminen, Valjakka, Erkkilä, Välkki,
Savonlinna Opera Festival C & O, Söderblom. F 1576-51101-2 (FACD 101)(1975/1990).
- *Kullervo* Op. 61. Hynninen, Saarinen, Salminen, Silvasti,
Finnish National Opera C & O, Söderblom. ODE 780-3T 3 CD (1992).
- *Rauta-aika-sarja* (The Iron Age Suite) Op. 55. Puupponen, East Helsinki Music
Institute Choir, Opera Festival Chorus, Helsinki PO, Kamu. ODE 844-2 (1995).

Sibelius, Jean
- *Karelia* JS 115
1) Laitinen, Hoffren, Laukka, Tiihonen, Lahti SO, Vänskä. BIS 915 (1997).
2) Virkkala, Liedes, Kotilainen, Tampere PO, Ollila. ODE 913-2 (1998).
(+ Sanomalehdistön päivän musiikkia JS 137)
- *Kullervo* Op. 7
1) Hynninen, Groop, The Polytech Choir, Finnish RSO, Saraste. F 0630-14906-2(1996).
2) Laukka, Paasikivi, YL, Lahti SO, Vänskä. BIS 1215 (2001).
- *Kyllikki* Op. 41. Eero Heinonen. F 8573-80772-2 (2000).
- *Laulu Lemminkäiselle* (A Song for Lemminkäinen) Op. 31 No 1.
Finnish National Opera C & O, Klas. ODE 754-2 (2000). (+ Väinön virsi)
- *Lemminkäinen-sarja* (Lemminkäinen Suite) Op. 22. Swedish RSO, Franck.
ODE 953-2 (2000). (+ En saga Op. 9)
- *Luonnotar* Op. 70. Isokoski, Sibelius Academy SO, Davis.
Sibelius Academy SACD 13 (2000).
- *Pohjolan tytär* (Pohjola's Daughter) Op. 49
1) LSO, Kajanus. F 3984-22155-2 (1932/1998).
2) CBSO, Oramo. Erato 8573-85822-2 (2001). (+ Karelia-sarja)
3) Lahti SO, Vänskä. BIS 1225 (2002). (+ En saga Op. 9)
- *Sanomalehdistön päivän musiikkia* (Press Celebrations Music) JS 137
1) Virkkala, Liedes, Kotilainen, Tampere PO and Choir, Ollila.
ODE 913-2 (1998). (+ Karelia)
2) Pöysti, Helsinki University Chorus (YL), Lahti Boys' Choir,
Lahti SO, Vänskä. BIS 1115 (2000).
- *En saga* Op. 9
1) [Original 1892 version]. Lahti SO, Vänskä. BIS 800 (1995).
2) Swedish RSO, Franck. ODE 953-2 (2000). (+ Lemminkäinen-sarja)
3) Lahti SO, Vänskä. BIS 1225 (2002). (+ Pohjolan tytär)
- *Tapiola* Op. 112
1) Helsinki PO, Beecham. ODE 809-2 (1954/1993).
2) Lahti SO, Vänskä. BIS 864 (1997).
3) Finnish RSO, Berglund. F 0927-46663-2 (1968/2002).
- *Tiera* JS 200. The Finnish Brass Ensemble, Saraste. Alba ABCD 102 (1994).
- *Tulen synty* (The Origin of Fire) Op. 32. Tiilikainen, Laulun Ystävät Male Choir,
Gothenburg SO, N. Järvi. BIS 314 (1986).

- *Väinön virsi* (Väinö's Song) Op. 110. Finnish National Opera C & O, Klas. ODE 754-2 (2000). (+ Laulu Lemminkäiselle)
- *Choral collections*
1) Works for Male Choir. YL, Hyökki. F FACD 205S (1987). [incl. *Terve kuu* (Hail, moon) Op. 18/2; *Rakastava* (The Lover) Op. 14; *Saarella palaa* (Fire on the Island) Op. 18/4; *Sortunut ääni* (The Broken Voice) Op. 18/1, and *Venematka* (The Boat Journey) Op. 18/3]
2) Complete Choral Songs for Mixed, Female and Children's Voices. Tapiola Chamber Choir & Friends of Sibelius, Norjanen. F 0630-19054-2 (1998). [Incl. *Min rastas raataa* (The Thrush's Toiling) JS 129; *Rakastava* (The Lover) Op. 14; *Saarella palaa* (Fire on the Island) Op. 18/4; *Soitapas, soria likka* (Play a Tune, O Fairest Maiden) JS 176; *Sortunut ääni* (The Broken Voice) Op. 18/1, and *Venematka* (The Boat Journey) Op. 18/3]

Tuomela, Tapio
- *Tuli tuuli, tuli aalto...* (Lamentation). Viljakainen, Finnish National Opera O, Tuomela. JaseCD 0031 (1999).

Other Kalevala Compilations

Kalevala sävelissä (Kalevala in Sounds)
Jean Sibelius: *Tapiola* Op. 121; *Venematka* Op. 18/3; *Terve kuu* Op. 18/2; *Kullervo* Op. 7 (excerpt); **Heikki Sarmanto:** *Kalevala Fantasy* 'Passions of a man'; **Uuno Klami:** *Kalevala Suite* Op. 23; **Einojuhani Rautavaara:** *Marjatta, matala neiti*. Various performers. Previously released material. F 3984-23856-2 (1999).

Further reading

www.fimic.fi > Contemporary Music
– The site contains over 150 composer pages dedicated mostly to contemporary composers as well as articles on the history of Finnish classical music and several publications on Finnish classical music.

IV

Kalevala poetry in Finnish jazz

Petri Silas

It says a lot about the jazz tastes of Scandinavia that the best-selling jazz disc in the region is *Jazz på svenska* [Jazz in Swedish] recorded by pianist **Jan Johansson** in the early 1960s. This disc, which has sold over 250,000 copies in Sweden alone, features meditative performances of Swedish folk songs. At about the same time, Finnish jazz musicians too began to seek inspiration in our folk tradition and, ultimately, in the *Kalevala* itself.

Karelia and Piirpauke blaze the trail

The first major step towards the treasury of the *Kalevala* was taken by a band named **Karelia,** founded in 1970 by guitarist **Ilpo 'Ilja' Saastamoinen** (b. 1942) and three musicians who already had a track record of being in the vanguard of aesthetic anarchy in Finnish jazz: saxophonist **Seppo 'Baron' Paakkunainen** (b. 1943), drummer **Edward Vesala** (1945–1999) and bass player **Pekka Sarmanto** (b. 1945). Karelia combined the melodies and rhythms of folk music, the energy of rock and the improvisation of jazz in a style unprecedented in this country.

The band's repertoire consisted mostly of old Finnish folk tunes, often in highly innovative arrangements following the trends of fusion jazz, which had emerged in the late 1960s. The electric storm conjured up by Karelia compares easily with **Fairport Convention** and **Jethro Tull** in the British Isles; Karelia was frequently too much for folk music purists, but that never bothered the band members.

A direct link with the national epic showed itself in the monikers adopted by the band members, a nod towards the *runo* singers perpetuating the oral tradition:

Sakari Kukko (B. 1953) IS THE FOUNDER OF *Piirpauke*, WHICH CELEBRATED ITS 30TH ANNIVERSARY IN 2004. THE BAND IS DISTINGUISHED FOR ITS BLEND OF JAZZ AND VARIOUS TYPES OF FOLK MUSIC. WE MIGHT EVEN SAY THAT PIIRPAUKE WAS PERFORMING WORLD MUSIC BEFORE THE TERM HAD EVEN BEEN INVENTED. PHOTO: MAARIT KYTÖHARJU / FIMIC.

e.g. Vesala was billed as Iivana Nyhtänköljä and Paakkunainen as Armas Nukarainen. Karelia released the albums *Suomi Pop* and *Suomi Pop 2* in 1970–1972. The début album includes *Peltoniemen Hintrikin surumarssi* (The Funeral March of Hintriki Peltoniemi), which acquired subsequent international fame when the **Kronos Quartet** recorded the Third String Quartet of **Aulis Sallinen** (b. 1935), based on that same tune, in 1986. Paakkunainen's début solo album *Nunnu* (1971) also features members of Karelia. This acclaimed album alone demonstrated what profound insights Paakkunainen had into the Finnish folk tradition, while also laying a foundation for his career, which is still going strong.

Karelia never became a hit with the public at large. Its successor in this field, on the other hand, managed to conquer the airwaves with one particular folk music arrangement that became an evergreen of sorts. This was, of course, *Konevitsan kirkonkellot* (Church Bells of Konevitsa) from the eponymous début album (1975) of **Piirpauke**.

Piirpauke, still active and still led by saxophonist **Sakari Kukko** (b. 1935), was founded in 1974. It sought a profile based on the freedom of the jazz idiom and rhythmic and harmonic devices derived from the folk music of various traditions. In retrospect, it has been said that Piirpauke was doing pure-bred 'world music' before the term had even been invented. Kukko and his colleagues, such as guitarist **Hasse Walli** (b. 1948) and bass player **Antti Hytti** (b. 1950), attained popularity in continental Europe too in the mid-1970s.

Large-scale works

In the early 1970s, the left-wing song movement, very strong elsewhere in Europe, arrived in Finland. The time-honoured tradition of defeating one's opponent in song was here championed by **Eero Ojanen** (b. 1943), **Toni Edelmann** (b. 1945) and **Kaj Chydenius** (b. 1939). The first of these drew upon the *Kalevala* as well as upon political ideology: Ojanen's cantata *Väinämöisen soitto* (Väinämöinen's Music) was premiered at the Pori Jazz Festival in summer 1974. The main inspiration behind the piece was the 40th *Runo* in the Kalevala, where Väinämöinen fashions a kantele out of the jawbone of a pike.

In 1976, ex-Karelia members revisited the world of the *Kalevala*: Saastamoinen recorded his album *Joutsenen juju* (The Swan's Trick), and Paakkunainen wrote the music for the stage play *Kanteletar* at the Helsinki City Theatre, named after and based on stories from the collection of lyrical poetry forming a companion to the *Kalevala*.

Both men returned to this material time and time again in the late 1970s and early 1980s. Saastamoinen's next major work in this area was the *Kalevala Suite*, which the Kajaani Big Band premiered in its entirety in 1980. Paakkunainen also showed shades of the *Kalevala* tradition in his work and was beginning his collaboration with yoik master **Nils-Aslak Valkeapää** (1943–2001) around this time.

As the 1980s rolled in, Piirpauke was still alive and well, and the rumours of the death of Karelia proved to be much exaggerated. This time around, a strong contribution to the band's sound was made by keyboard player **Esa Kotilainen** (b. 1946). The best recordings from this period were *Tuohihuilu / The Sound of Birchbark Flute* (1981) and *Maanitus* (1983).

Vesala took up the torch in 1986 when he completed his radio play and album *Kullervo*, based on a story from the *Kalevala*. In the previous year, Paakkunainen had created music for a stage play entitled *Kalevala*, directed by Paavo Liski. We may safely say that, even at this relatively early stage, both men had been solidly captured by the enchantment of the *Kalevala*.

Kukko and Vesala: multiculturalism and deeper shamanism

Piirpauke continued on its chosen path, travelling from the Balkans to Bagdad and from Morocco to Mumbai. But as certain track titles (e.g. *Kantele* and *Rannalla istuja* [Sitter on the Shore]) and the variation on the painting *Sammon taonta* (Forging of the Sampo, 1893) by **Akseli Gallen-Kallela (1865–1931)** chosen for the cover of the album *The Wild East* (1986) demonstrate, the influence of Finnish culture and the *Kalevala* acted as a stabilizing anchor in the increasingly multicultural soundscape of the band.

The selection of that particular painting as an album cover may have had something to do with the 150th anniversary of our national epic in 1985. The *Kalevala* anniversary manifested itself in the Finnish arts in many ways. For instance, the City of Kajaani commissioned a piece from Sakari Kukko. This piece, *Väinämöisen soitto* (Väinämöinen's Music), may be found not only on the album *The Wild East* but also on the album *Kalevala Spirit*, which Piirpauke released in 2000. The latter also includes other material paying homage to the runo singers of Karelia and Ingria.

At the same time, the work of Edward Vesala acquired almost folk-education proportions with the founding of his legendary **Sound & Fury** workshop and orchestra. The Sound & Fury workshop was not only a flexible laboratory and

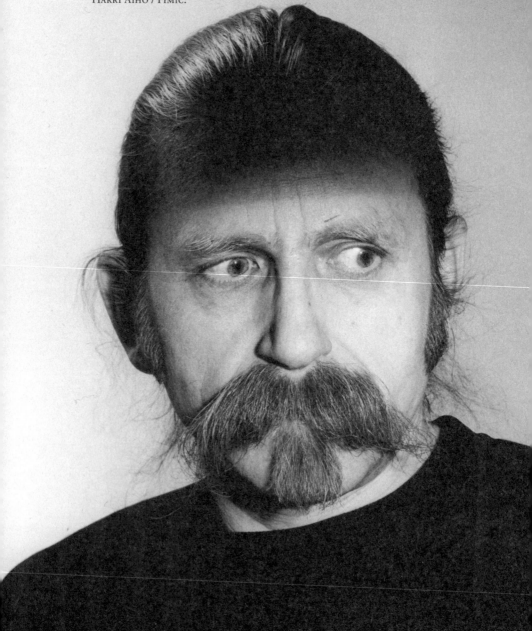

Edward Vesala (1945–1999) was one of the most shaman-like musicians in Finnish jazz. His *Sound & Fury* band achieved the peak of its career in the classic modern European jazz albums *Lumi* (Snow, 1987) and *Ode to the Death of Jazz* (1990). Photo: Harri Aiho / Fimic.

orchestra for Vesala but also a touring educational unit that gave numerous school concerts. The Finnish flavour remained strong in his work to the end, and the presence of a kind of *Kalevala* undercurrent culminated in two discs released by ECM that have since been recognized as classics of modern European jazz: *Lumi* (Snow, 1987) and *Ode to the Death of Jazz* (1990).

Vesala's workshop was the springboard for many of the most highly regarded and most uncompromising Finnish jazz musicians of today, such as **Raoul Björkenheim** (b. 1956), **Tapani Rinne** (b. 1962), **Pertti 'Pepa' Päivinen** (b. 1955) and **Iro Haarla** (b. 1956), all disciples of Vesala's in the late 1980s and early 1990s.

It seems almost trivial to describe Edward Vesala as a shaman in an age when anyone sticking a bit of shallow tribalism or anything remotely resembling a chant into his music is immediately heralded as a shaman. But there was, nevertheless, something primeval and inexorably powerful in this tenacious monolith of a musician.

Sarmanto and Pohjola: symphonic works and a strong Finnish flavour

Our other significant and internationally noted jazz composer, **Heikki Sarmanto** (b. 1939), finally had his major work *Kalevala Fantasy* recorded in the early 1990s. Typically for his style, the piece is massive, narrative and quite literally poetic. Its first version was completed in 1986, but it was not until five years later that it was released, in an excellent performance by UMO Jazz Orchestra. It is a work ambitious in scale, like many of Sarmanto's compositions; its roots lie equally in jazz, classical music and Finnish literature. Sarmanto is highly regarded by his colleagues too: around the time of this release, saxophonist Pentti Lahti in an interview for *Rytmi* magazine praised the *Kalevala*-like melodic writing of Sarmanto.

Measured by the number of recordings released, the early 1990s were a fairly quiet period in Finnish jazz, but towards the end of the millennium the scene brightened up considerably. Some newcomers produced music that could be traced back to the *Kalevala*, but some old-timers made fine music as well.

Composer and bass player **Pekka Pohjola** (b. 1952) had been exploring the juncture of rock, jazz and classical music since the 1970s. In the mid-1990s, he put together a splendid new band called **Pekka Pohjola Group** and cut the brilliant albums *Heavy Jazz * Live in Helsinki and Tokyo* (1995) and *Pewit* (1997). The rugged Sibelian Finnishness of his music found excellent performers in pianist **Seppo Kantonen** (b. 1963), guitarist **Markku Kanerva** (b. 1965) and drummer **Anssi Nykänen** (b. 1965), even though the composer himself never could explain why his music seemed so archetypally Finnish. In an interview for the *Soundi* rock magazine, he did hint at subconscious indoctrination: being the child of a culturally enlightened family, he had been intrigued since childhood by the 'Great Kalevala' illustrated by Gallen-Kallela, which was constantly on display in his home.

End of the millennium: a new generation

Of the recent newcomers, the most obviously Finnish in his music is pianist **Samuli Mikkonen** (b. 1973). His albums *Korpea kuunnellessa* (Listening to the Wilderness, 1998) and *Samuli Mikkonen & 7 henkeä* (Samuli Mikkonen & 7 Spirits, 2003) referred to the idiom of Edward Vesala in terms of arrangements and thematic development but also further back to the *Kalevala*, an important influence for Vesala too. The very first track on Mikkonen's début album is a nod towards the national epic, being titled *Raudan synty* (The Origin of Iron). Apart from leading his own bands, Mikkonen has also been involved in an orchestra named **Wäinämöiset**. Saxophonist **Pekka Toivanen** (b. 1961), whose album *Kantelettaren parhaat* (The Best of the Kanteletar) was released in 1999, also draws on ancient poetry.

There was also a hint of the *Kalevala* in the concerts of a large ensemble named **Suhkan Uhka**. A joint effort by old hands such as saxophonist **Juhani Aaltonen** (b. 1935) and bass player Antti Hytti and young virtuosos such as trumpet player

Verneri Pohjola (b. 1977), the band released its début album *Suhka* in 2003. The disc features a fine *Kalevala* piece, *Tuonen tytti* (Death's Maiden), by Hytti and the other leading figure of the band, saxophonist **Jouni 'Jone' Takamäki** (b. 1955).

It is sometimes observed that the Bible occupies the place on Finnish tables today that the *Kalevala* did in the 19th century, at the height of the nationalist movement and its reflections in the fine arts and music. The ancient pagan folk religion and its manifestations in the folk tradition still manifest themselves today, sometimes in surprising contexts.

In jazz, the most recent example of this was the 300th anniversary of the 'Old Hymnal' of 1701 in 2001. The 'hymn boom' that took off around that time generated a number of high-quality discs such as *Virret* (Hymns, 2002) by Sakari Kukko, *Kaanaanmaa* (Canaan, 2002) by saxophonist **Jukka Perko** (b. 1968) and *Piae Cantiones* (2002) by guitarist **Niklas Winter** (b. 1969). It is difficult to believe that any of these discs could have been anywhere near as gripping if their creators had not grown up with our national epic, compiled by Elias Lönnrot.

Select discography & Further reading

- **Seppo Paakkunainen:** *Nunnu* (1971). BLUE MASTER SPECIAL SPEL 301 (LP).
- **Piirpauke:** *Piirpauke* (1975). LOVE RECORDS LRCD 148.
- **Piirpauke:** *Villi itä* (THE WILD EAST) (1987). ROCKADILLO ZENCD 2004, JARO GERMANY 4150-2.
- **Vesala Sound & Fury:** *Lumi* (1986). ECM 1339.
- **Vesala Sound & Fury:** *Ode to the Death of Jazz* (1989). ECM 1413.
- **Samuli Mikkonen:** *Samuli Mikkonen & 7 henkeä* (2003). SMCD 3.
- **Suhkan Uhka:** *Suhka* (2003). TUM RECORDS TUMCD 001.

www.fimic.fi > Jazz
- The site contains dozens of composer and artist pages as well as an article on the history of Finnish jazz by Petri Silas.

Piirpauke: www.rockadillo.fi/piirpauke/

V

Kalevala poetry in Finnish popular music

Hannu Tolvanen:

On the Kalevala tradition in Finnish popular music before the 1970s

The *Kalevala* tradition was of minor importance in Finnish popular music until the 1970s, and even since then music based (even loosely) on the national epic has scarcely put in an appearance in the Top 20. Although the ancient tradition, thousands of years old, does not seem to have lent itself readily to popular music, some of its features are part and parcel of the very essence of Finnish popular music. We might even say that the *Kalevala* maintains an unnoticed yet pervasive presence in it.

Kalevala elements in Finnish popular music

To generalize, the main musical features of the *Kalevala* tradition are 5/4 metre and melodies based on a minor-key pentachord. Popular music, on the other hand, is typically in duple metre, and 5/4 is too complicated. But pentatonic melodies are easy enough to use; after all, pentatonic scales are known all over the world.

In *Kalevala* chants, the melodic profile is like a waveform, a phrase beginning on the fundament and usually descending back to it. Such descending pentatonic melodic profiles can be found in the vast majority of recent Finnish popular music. Studies on Finnish hit songs have shown that a descending minor-key pentachord is one of their most typical characteristics. The melancholy of the descending fifth chimes with typically Finnish gloomy moods.

Alliteration is a poetic device that features heavily in the *Kalevala* and has persisted in Finnish literature and music of all styles and periods. Through the decades, it has been an important feature in popular music too.

By contrast, the linear nature of *Kalevala* chants (no refrains) is at variance with forms of popular music, although epic continuous narratives are by no means unknown in Finnish pop music. Also, lyrics in the popular music of western Europe and North America tend to rhyme, and rhymes are all but unknown in *Kalevala* poetry. Another feature of *Kalevala* poetry that is difficult to employ in popular music is the structural device of placing the longest word in each line at its end.

The emergence of popular music: the music of cities and a new breed of tradition

The development of Finnish popular music in the 19th century is related to the general European transition brought on by industrialization and urbanization, which profoundly affected social structures all over Europe. To simplify, we might say that the very concept of popular music and its emergence in Finland is synonymous with the abandoning of the *runo* singing of the *Kalevala*.

The new popular music was the music of the urban bourgeoisie and as such heralded a new world view and a new society considerably different from the rural communities that gave birth to the runo singing tradition. Early popular music drew on folk music — dance music in particular — but on a stratum which was more recent than the *Kalevala* tradition and which had already taken on the shape of European models. Generally speaking, when we discuss folk music influences in Finnish popular music from the 19th century up to the 1970s, we refer to the more recent stratum of rhymed stanzaic songs rather than the ancient *runo* singing tradition.

It is illustrative of the transition period of the 19th century that while popular music in cities diverged from the ancient tradition, **Elias Lönnrot** (1802–1884) compiled the national epic, the *Kalevala* (1835 and 1849), and thus elevated the old mythology into a figurehead for official Finnish culture and Finnishness. Compiling the *Kalevala* into book form, into a poetry collection that one might read, represented a literalization of the previously oral tradition and coincides with a time at which the musical content of the tradition began to be forgotten. Although this musical idiom remained in living memory in Karelia well into the 20th century, in more populated areas it disappeared and ceased to be an element in the official culture.

Also at the same time, Finnish music began to orient itself more closely with the classical music of central Europe with the first performances in Finland of operas by Mozart, Rossini and von Weber. The first *Kalevala*-based concert works dating from the mid-19th century were firmly rooted in the European classical tradition in terms of their musical idiom, and it was not until the end of the 19th century that **Jean Sibelius** (1865–1957) made the first serious attempts to blend ancient *runo* singing into classical music.

Proliferation of musical life

In 1809, Finland became an autonomous Grand Duchy in the Russian Empire. Russian influences soon appeared in Finnish music too: the Russian waltz-romance had a decisive impact on Finnish popular music. The ascending minor sixth, a characteristic interval in Russian tunes, is to this day an important feature in Finnish popular music.

The 19th century also saw a proliferation of musical life in towns. Restaurants with salon orchestras that might have up to 20 members became commonplace. The repertoire of such orchestras usually consisted of European classical music. Towards the end of the century, civic organizations began to arise in towns and smaller industrial communities. The purpose of these organizations was to coordinate the increasing leisure time of workers, and music played an important part in this. Performances by choirs and brass septets became highlights of the entertainments of workers' associations, youth societies, volunteer fire brigades and temperance societies. These amateur ensembles performed popular classics and stanzaic folk songs in a variety of arrangements.

The *Kalevala* yielded material for recitation, a clear indication that not only was the music associated with this poetic tradition considered unfashionable, it had also disappeared. Solemn recitations of the *Kalevala* also demonstrated that the original function of the traditional poetry — entertainment — had been replaced by edification, art, national sentiment and high culture.

The 'coupleteers'

The turn of the 20th century was a lively and international period in the major cities of Helsinki, Turku and Viipuri. Finland was treated to glimpses of the newest European musical trends as numerous entertainers passed through the land en route to St. Petersburg, the metropolis at the eastern end of the Gulf of Finland.

The most original genre in Finnish popular music in the early 20th century was that practiced by the 'coupleteers', itinerant restaurant singers whose ditties were often variations on Finnish folk songs. Some 'coupleteers' retained a tenuous link to the ancient Finnish tradition in that **Pasi Jääskeläinen (1869–1920)** and **Olli Suolahti** (1885–1951), for instance, accompanied themselves on the kantele. This remained the last direct reference to the world of the *Kalevala* in Finnish popular music until the 1970s.

The kantele never really went away, though, since after all it is our national instrument. Kantele performances by **Ulla Katajavuori** (1909–2001) in particular were frequently broadcast in the 1950s, but we should note that the music programming of the Finnish Broadcasting Company, which was founded in the late 1920s, included a considerably larger proportion of folk music and folk songs than was featured in Finnish films or on Finnish recordings, for instance. We should note that kantele music on the radio at that time followed the then current thinking on folk music, and the instrument was never used outside its proper genre.

Noisy jazz, mambo and translated schlagers

The influence of the later stratum of folk songs on popular music also diminished as the 20th century progressed. Increasingly, influences in popular music came from central Europe and North America. The buzzwords of the 1920s and 1930s were 'noisy jazz', 'salon jazz', 'hot' and, ultimately, 'accordion jazz'; the leading dance music ensemble of the day was the **Dallapé Orchestra**. Its influences were basically American, though the brilliance and musical experimentation of jazz proper were lacking. The rumba, the samba, the conga, the mambo and the cha-cha became popular in the 1950s, and Finnish popular music in this decade was characterized by National Romantic rustic ditties on one hand and schlagers translated into Finnish on the other.

Jazzy schlagers were a key import in the 1950s, and through these a great many new, fresh women artists appeared on the popular music scene. Rock also arrived in Finland, although the first Finnish versions of **Bill Haley's** *Rock around the clock* were actually quick foxes rather than rock. Huge numbers of guitar bands sprang up in Finland in the 1960s, and the upbeat version of the old folk song *Emma* recorded by **The Sounds** became hugely popular, selling tens of thousands of copies and being known as far afield as in Japan.

Emma is yet another case in point showing that popular music might make use of folk songs but not the runo singing of the *Kalevala*.

Why not until the 1970s?

Why did the *Kalevala* and its heritage not appear in Finnish popular music until the 1970s? Why was it that experimental, broad-minded jazz and rock musicians were the ones to rediscover this tradition in popular music?

In the 1960s, jazz and rock musicians began to explore new avenues. The end of the decade in particular marked an intense search for new things, and in both rock and jazz influences were sought in modern classical music and in other cultures. Finally, a few musicians ended up looking to our own folk tradition — following the model of musicians in other countries exploring theirs. The *Kalevala* tradition never did settle into the metrically, rhythmically, harmonically and textually rather standardized world of popular music as a conscious element; the '*Kalevala* features' referred to at the beginning of this article exist in Finnish popular music as a hidden and subconscious layer.

In considering the popular music of the 1970s based on the *Kalevala* heritage, it is interesting to note that the phenomenon emerged and developed in the more experimental margins of popular music. It is also interesting that the first experiments became highly popular: the tracks gained a lot of air time on radio, and they even reached the charts. Ancient *runo* singing became for certain musicians a basic philosophy and source of inspiration that coloured their entire subsequent careers. For audiences, this music reaching back into an age-old tradition and shades of shamanism was new in terms of both material and treatment, showing the ancient mainstream in an almost avant-garde light, a sort of secret lore sung forth by a modern-day Väinämöinen.

Further reading

Pekka Jalkanen: *The roots of Finnish popular music*
www.fimic.fi > Folk and World Music > History
- The article describes the beginnings of Finnish popular music
and its Central European and Slavic influences.

Petri Silas:
The Kalevala and prog rock

When progressive rock was in its ascendancy in the British Isles in the late 1960s, it was characterized by the sort of pomp usually associated with classical music and by escapist fantasy in its lyrics. However, although many lyricists cited the *Lord of the Rings* trilogy by **J.R.R. Tolkien** (1892–1973) as their inspiration, very few were savvy enough to trace these influences even further back to one of Tolkien's major sources of inspiration: the *Kalevala*.

'Prog rock' quickly found proponents and a fan base in Finland. The best and brightest bands, **Wigwam** and **Tasavallan Presidentti**, were founded on the ruins of the recently deceased **Blues Section** in 1969. Tasavallan Presidentti (the name translates as President of the Republic) played music in a generic European style, while Wigwam, particularly in the early stages of its career, made strong references to its Finnish roots.

Wigwam was initially very much a double act between keyboard player and singer **Jim Pembroke** (b. 1946) and keyboard player **Jukka Gustavson** (b. 1951). The most '*Kalevala*-oriented' band member was bass player **Mats Huldén** (b. 1949), who authored the band's only track that could be conceivably be classified as '*Kalevala* style', the shamanist chant *Häätö* (Banishment), a single from 1970 with Gustavson's *Pedagogi* as its B side. Huldén also designed the band's album cover art for a long time.

Another viewpoint on our national epic was brought to Wigwam by bass player **Pekka Pohjola** (b. 1952), who played with the band from 1970 to 1974. On the classic album *Nuclear Nightclub* (1975), Wigwam's sound was broadened by the addition of a connoisseur of various ethnic musical traditions, keyboard player **Esa Kotilainen** (b. 1946). One should not imagine, however, that Pohjola and Kotilainen always flavoured their performances with patriotic or *Kalevala* flavours, but a certain primeval Finnish seriousness and stolidity, as well as the sort of playfulness typical of the culture of Karelia (the collecting place of the *Kalevala*), can be identified.

In 1972, a band named **Kalevala** released its début album, with tracks mainly by guitarist **Matti Kurkinen** (1951–1975). Despite the band's name, however, the sturdy prog rock of the band contains scarcely anything that could be associated with the national epic.

For some reason, the *Kalevala* has been left untouched in Finnish prog rock since the 1970s. We should note, however, that this long-outmoded genre has risen back into the echelons of mainstream popular music during the past decade or so.

In one sense, the relationship between the *Kalevala* and musicians came full circle in 1999 when Mats Huldén and his father Lars Huldén completed a new Swedish translation of the *Kalevala*.

We should also mention the triple CD *Kalevala — A Finnish Progressive Rock Epic* released in 2003. Here, 30 emerging European prog rock musicians explore themes and tunes inspired by the *Kalevala*. The disc was conceived by the Colossus prog rock association founded in Helsinki in 1995, and it was released under the French label Musea, which specializes in art rock.

Select discography & Further reading

Wigwam: *Fresh Garbage - Wigwam Rarities* (2000). LOVE RECORDS LXCD 626.

Wigwam: members.surfeu.fi/mmerilai/wigwam/

Wigwam, ONE OF THE PIONEERS OF FINNISH PROGRESSIVE ROCK, WAS THE MOST CONSPICUOUS IN ITS GENRE IN ITS USE OF NATIONAL ELEMENTS. THE *Kalevala* TRADITION MADE A CAMEO APPEARANCE IN THE PIECE *Häätö* (BANISHMENT, 1970). WIGWAM MEMBERS (CLOCKWISE, FROM TOP LEFT) **Jukka Gustavson, Pekka Pohjola, Ronnie Österberg** AND **Jim Pembroke.** PHOTOS: JORMA AUERSALO.

Samuli Knuuti:

"It's the language, you see." The importance of the Kalevala in contemporary Finnish rock

The *Kalevala* and modern rock music? How could they possibly have anything in common? A folk epic in archaic language and a noisy breed of music often derided for being supranational?

It is, admittedly, difficult to find direct links between the *Kalevala* and, for instance, the rock albums in Finnish that topped the charts last week. A list of pieces retelling the tale of Kullervo or the stealing of the Sampo within the 3.5-minute confines of a pop song will inevitably remain very short indeed. Only in the progressive rock of the 1970s and in recent heavy metal music can we find direct thematic connections to the mythology of the *Kalevala* — and both these genres are discussed elsewhere in this book.

So, does the absence of direct references mean that the Finnish national epic is simply of no importance in modern rock music? The answer is a resounding 'no'. But justifying this answer is a tough call, relying largely on intuition.

Unique relationship of rock lyrics to literature

It cannot be an accident that lyrics have always occupied a position of central importance in Finnish rock culture. Finnish rock musicians have demonstrated an exceptionally close relationship to literature. **Kauko Röyhkä** (b. 1959), **Pelle Miljoona** (b. 1955), **A.W. Yrjänä** (of **CMX**; b. 1966), **Tuomari Nurmio** (b. 1950) and **Tommi Liimatta** (singer with **Absoluuttinen Nollapiste**; b. 1976) are but a few upstanding Finnish rock artists who have also published literary works, either prose or poetry.

These literary works are not even related to the lyrics of their authors, which also have been compiled and published both as single-artist collections and as thematic anthologies. The cream of the crop in Finnish rock lyricists qualifies as a subject of literary criticism studies in universities alongside contemporary poets; indeed, many consider that in the late 1990s the rock lyricist supplanted the contemporary poet. This situation is very different from that of the mainstream of Anglo-Saxon rock music, where quality lyrics that stand scrutiny as poetry in their own right without the music are in extremely short supply.

There must be something behind this; there must be a reason why lyrics have always been held in high esteem in Finland. Why not go way back in time to find out, right back to the days of the *Kalevala*?

Of course, it would be laying it on with a trowel to claim that all Finnish contemporary rock music with snazzy lyrics is based on the *runo* singing tradition of the *Kalevala*! Naturally, the main influences for image and music particularly in mainstream Finnish rock come from international models rather than the homegrown tradition. Besides, the very best Finnish pop lyricists defy categorization: there is a world of difference for example between the wittily rhymed melancholy of **Eppu Normaali** and the mythological, opaque lyrics of CMX, or between the acerbic vernacular everyday drama of **Zen Café** and the reckless surrealism of Tuomari Nurmio.

Runo singing in rock: the demand for good lyrics

What binds Finnish lyricists to roots harking back to the *Kalevala* is the **demand** on part of the audience for a certain level of quality in lyrics: this is a fundamental requirement for a band to even dream of being successful. Finnish audiences expect rock singers to tell stories, four-minute novellas as it were, where the music can function more as a vehicle for the narrative than as the main focus of attention. Of course, audiences do not expect *all* artists to produce lyrics of such quality — it is entirely possible to be a hit in Finland with lyrics that are not so great — but there is a special niche at the cutting edge of Finnish rock for good, strong lyricists.

In order for a rock song to be memorable, it must — audiovisual technology notwithstanding — abide by the same repetition rules and qualitative requirements as the poetry of the *Kalevala*. It is not enough that a song can be played off a disc at any time — listeners must *want* to hear it again and again. Like the *runo* singers of the 19th century, modern-day rock artists must be able both to adapt and vary the tradition and to repeat what they have learned, even though the traditions involved are of course very different.

This connection is seen and acknowledged by **Heikki Laitinen** (b. 1943), Professor of Folk Music at the Sibelius Academy, who in his extensive and meritorious history of Finnish rock music, *Jee Jee Jee* (1998), wrote: "The majority of Finnish rock poets are direct descendants if not of folk poets then of Lauri Viita and other poets who wrote rhyming verse and who in turn drew inspiration from folk songs. There is a definite continuum. It's the language, you see."

In addition to this fundamental tone that can only be observed indirectly, there are of course Finnish rock artists that demonstrate an overt link to the national epic.

Ismo Alanko, heir to the shamans

Ismo Alanko (b. 1960) has a quarter century at the top of Finnish rock music under his belt, first as the leader of the bands **Hassisen kone** and **Sielun veljet** and subsequently as a solo artist. He even looks like he could have stepped out of a *Kalevala* painting by Akseli Gallen-Kallela: his bony features and coarse blond hair would make him suitable to play either the maltreated Kullervo or the errant hero Lemminkäinen. Alanko has also cultivated a manic style of singing and performing to create a shamanist impression, and this has become one of his trademarks.

One of Alanko's favourite devices as a lyricist is to mix images from ancient Finnish poetry to trendy contemporary language, creating an ironic mishmash. A well-known case in point is *Kun Suomi putos puusta* (When Finland fell out of a tree,

1990), aiming to depict the Finn of the late 1980s who had "one foot in the cow-shed and the other on the tennis court, one hand holding an udder and the other a remote control". Its lyrics display a deliciously incongruous blend of *Kalevala* scansion and modern vocabulary. Indeed, Ismo Alanko uses *Kalevala* themes and allusions as a sort of tool to illustrate the collision of ancient Finnish culture and chaotic modern times while satirizing both, albeit satirizing modern times more.

Ismo Alanko (MIDDLE) MAKES A HABIT OF PLAYING AROUND WITH DIFFERENT LEVELS OF LANGUAGE. ON HIS ALBUM *Kun Suomi putos puusta* (WHEN FINLAND FELL OUT OF A TREE, 1990), THE JUXTAPOSITION OF ANCIENT POETRY AND MODERN CONCEPTS TRANSLATES INTO INCISIVE IRONY. PHOTO: NAUSKA / POKO REKORDS.

CMX and primeval alliteration

CMX, one of the most important Finnish rock bands of the 1990s, also draws on ancient Finnish culture, and indeed the titles of their albums often allude subtly to the mythology of the *Kalevala*. The title of *Rautakantele* (Iron Kantele, 1995) embodies a fusion of a traditional instrument and heavy metal, while *Vainajala* (1998) seeks a parallel with Tuonela, the realm of the dead in the *Kalevala* (*vainaja* = dead person).

The lyrics of CMX are informed by an obvious consciousness of the potential of *Kalevala* poetry in rock music. An extreme example is *Timanttirumpu* (Diamond Drum, 1992), whose pithy text could have come straight from the Kanteletar: "venehellä vaskisella / kuutilla kuparisella / alisihin taivosihin / ylisihin maa-emihin" ("in a boat so bold and brazen / in a coracle of copper / to the lowest of the heavens / to the highest of the earth-lands"). More subtly, CMX lyrics are replete with ancient phrasings and avoid, particularly in the band's early output, modern vocabulary (or use it with acidic irony for satirical purposes, as Ismo Alanko does). CMX also break with the tradition of rhyming lyrics in popular music and instead resort to primeval Finnish alliteration. Ever argumentative, CMX have sought to belittle the importance of the *Kalevala* in their output: "We have maybe three songs where the lyrics are in *Kalevala* metre," says singer and lyricist A.W. Yrjänä dryly.

The *Kalevala* impression in CMX songs rests ultimately on the solemn and archaic tone of Yrjänä's lyrics. He often writes about strong, timeless contrasts: night and day, fire and water, death and birth, god and devil. These mythic archetypes are of course so common that they can be considered universal manifestations of the human psyche, and as such not uniquely within the domain of the *Kalevala* — particularly since Yrjänä, being an autodidact, mixes in influences from various religions and classics of world literature.

However, couched in the expressive and often archaic language used by Yrjänä, aiming beyond our modern reality, such images do conjure up a certain *Kalevala* atmosphere, which has rubbed off on many other bands that admire CMX and consider them an influence. Several other heavy rock bands such as **Mokoma** and **Kotiteollisuus** have taken up and further developed the mythic dimension of Yrjänä's lyrics, its uncompromising nature being a tantalizing option to the current postmodern climate that turns everything into irony and dilutes meaning.

THE *Kalevala*-LIKE ATMOSPHERE OF THE MUSIC OF **CMX** STEMS FROM THE SOLEMN ARCHAIC LYRICS OF **A.W. Yrjänä** (RIGHT). "WE'VE HAD MAYBE LIKE THREE SONGS IN THE *Kalevala* METRE," SAYS YRJÄNÄ HIMSELF, BUT THE STYLISTIC FEATURES OF THE ANCIENT FOLK POETRY PERVADE THE BAND'S ENTIRE OUTPUT. PHOTO: ARI TALUSÈN / EMI.

Mythic ruggedness amidst sky channels

Thus, there are links between modern Finnish rock music and the *Kalevala*, even if artists themselves are not necessarily aware of them. When rock music in Finnish seriously got going in the 1970s, the aim was to cut completely loose from the romantic language and imagery appropriated by Finnish schlagers. As a result, a mythic ruggedness that can be traced back to the *Kalevala* has become a major element of Finnish rock lyrics over the decades. Even though many musicians have never read the epic (and have slept through the classes in school where it was discussed), something of it has nevertheless rubbed off.

And this rubbing off is something of which we can never, fortunately, be completely free. One cannot banish the spectre of the *Kalevala* wholly no matter how many international music channels and Top 20 radio stations one sets up in this country. As long as pop music is being made in the Finnish language, the national epic will be looming on the sidelines, just beyond conscious awareness. And it can only be a question of time when the first of the Finnish artists riding the crest of hiphop discovers inspiration in the themes and rhythms of the *Kalevala*. That should be interesting...

Select discography & Further reading

- **Ismo Alanko:** *Kun Suomi putos puusta.* (1990). POKO REKORDS VELVECD-3.
- **Ismo Alanko:** *Alangolla. Ismo Alangon lauluja* (4 CDs) (1997). POKO REKORDS ISMOBOX.
- **CMX:** *Aurinko* (1992). HERODES/EMI 777-7 80752 2 (CD), 777-7 80752 1 (LP), 777-7 80752 4 (MC).
- **CMX:** *Aura* (1994). HERODES/EMI 7243-8 28592 2 (CD), 7243-8 28592 4 (MC).
- **CMX:** *Rautakantele* (1995). HERODES/EMI 7243-8 670382 (CD), 7243-8 32659 4 (MC).
- **CMX:** *Vainajala* (1998). HERODES/EMI 7243 4 97660 2 0.
- **Mokoma:** *Tämän maailman kuninkaan hovissa* (2004). CD SKR003.

www.fimic.fi > Popular Music
- The page contains several entires and links to the main artists in the field of Finnish pop and rock music as well as articles on history of Finnish rock and various genres of popular music.

Ismo Alanko: www.ismoalanko.com
CMX: www.njet.net/cmx

Matti Riekki:

FROM THE SMITHY OF ILMARINEN.
KALEVALA AND HEAVY METAL

Our national epic has had a considerable impact on Finnish heavy rock, whether in terms of purely musical values or in terms of external elements such as cover art or image. The reasons are obvious: the *Kalevala* and its ancillary materials constitute an unbeatable source of tragic and romantic stories excellently suited to pompous metal music. It is also a great tool with which adventurous rock music from this tiny country can distinguish itself in the world at large.

We might say that welding the *Kalevala* to heavy metal was the Finnish response to 'Viking metal', the Scandinavian concept that seeks inspiration in paganism and the ancient Nordic warrior tradition. The foremost and most long-lived proponent of the horned helmet brigade was the Swedish band **Bathory**, led by the now deceased **Tomas 'Quorthon' Forsberg** (1965–2004), active from the early 1980s. Whereas the Viking brand of heavy rock drew on manly bravado and the heat of battle, the Finnish variation had more to do with extreme melancholy and sorrow.

Amorphis: The marriage of Kalevala and metal

Powerfully mythological heavy metal redolent with the scent of pine forests and the atmosphere of the *Kalevala* is still alive and well in Finland, though it enjoyed its heyday in the mid-1990s. Around that time, the Helsinki band **Amorphis** began to explore the tales of Väinämöinen and other mythical figures in their albums.

The band's début album, *The Karelian Isthmus* (1993), was about swords and scimitars on a more general level, but the next album, *Tales From The Thousand Lakes* (1994), plunged deep into the myths of the Kalevala and coined the phrase

'*Kalevala* metal'. The lyrics on Tales were directly derived from the national epic in the excellent English translation by **Keith Bosley** (b. 1937). Amorphis upped the stakes on their next album Elegy (1996), whose lyrics came from the *Kanteletar*, the lyrical-poetry companion volume to the *Kalevala* (see p. 29).

Lyrics were not the only channel for *Kalevala* influences in the music of Amorphis. The band flavoured their pungent death metal with lullaby-like melody lines that owed a great deal to folk tunes. Their usually medium-tempo tracks also involved a repetitive drive that harked back to the lullabies of the ancient tradition. Or drinking songs, for that matter. The alternation of sweet and crude singing alluded to the ancient call-and-response singing tradition. *My Kantele*, on *Elegy*, became one of Amorphis's best-known tracks; it is as close to an electric rendition of our national instrument as one is likely to get.

Although a listener in, say, Turkey might well identify the intricate, melancholy-ridden melodies of Amorphis with an eastern culture, the combination of these with a rock-solid foundation creates a peculiarly Finnish sound. At once sensitive and powerful, Amorphis is something that one might imagine oneself listening to after a sauna bath on the shore of a placid lake — not an image usually associated with heavy metal. This recipe has proved a successful export too, since *Tales From The Thousand Lakes* remains to this day one of the best-selling Finnish metal discs abroad. Amorphis is most probably the internationally best-known Finnish heavy metal band, particularly in North America.

The legacy of Amorphis

Those following in the footsteps of Amorphis have not been quite so keen to take up the matter of the *Kalevala*. Perhaps Amorphis was an act too tough to follow. **Ensiferum** and **Moonsorrow**, also from the Helsinki area, have continued the successful melding of folk music with metal, although through a more general swords-and-pagans approach than through the *Kalevala* specifically. Of the two, Ensiferum comes closer to the national epic: even the cover art on its two albums (*Ensiferum*, 2001; *Iron*, 2004) features a white-bearded warrior

Amorphis HAS ESTABLISHED THE CONCEPT OF 'Kalevala METAL' WITH SEVERAL ALBUMS, BRINGING IT INTO THE GALLERY OF HEROIC MYTHOLOGIES IN HEAVY MUSIC. THE ALLUSIONS TO ANCIENT POETRY ARE NOT ACCIDENTAL OR HIDDEN STYLISTIC ALLUSIONS: FOR INSTANCE, *My Kantele* IS AN ELECTRICALLY UPDATED HOMAGE TO THE NATIONAL INSTRUMENT. PHOTO: JOUKO LEHTOLA / EMI.

closely resembling Väinämöinen the ancient shaman, and there is a two-track number on the début disc dedicated to him. Also, Ensiferum use the kantele in their mix of instruments.

Insomnium from Joensuu has released two acclaimed albums (*In The Halls Of Awaiting*, 2002; *Since The Day It All Came Down*, 2004) continuing in the footsteps of Amorphis, though more in terms of music than of lyrics. They too draw not so much on the national epic as on generic Finnish forest mythology. **Finntroll**, a band performing pagan stuff in Swedish, have gone the furthest in amalgamating folk music and heavy metal. Their utterly twisted 'foxtrot metal' draws on polka beats and beer-barrel carousing, a blend every bit as original as that devised by Amorphis.

It is scarcely surprising that the most direct route to *Kalevala* metal today was built on the foundation — or perhaps we should now say the graveyard — of Amorphis. Soloist **Pasi Koskinen** (b. 1972) left Amorphis in late summer 2004 to work with the **Ajattara** band. Performing rugged black metal in Finnish, the band has released three albums (*Itse* [Self], 2001; *Kuolema* [Death], 2003; *Tyhjyys* [Emptiness], 2004) with profoundly gloomy lyrics that scan remarkably well. The music too is not such a far cry from the atmosphere of the more bloodsoaked tales of the *Kalevala*.

Admittedly 'stealing the Sampo' is not a big thing in Finland today. With Finnish rock music making its great export breakthrough, the Kalevala is perhaps considered unduly non-universal for heavy metal. Now that bands such as **HIM** and **Nightwish** have established a permanent niche for Finnish heavy rock internationally, we may yet see a new generation of proud descendants of Väinämöinen emerging.

To return to Amorphis one last time: although the band have intentionally distanced themselves from the *Kalevala*, having explored that avenue to its full extent, their latest studio album *Far From The Sun* (2003) has the same symbol on the cover as Tales did nearly ten years earlier: the hammer of Ukko, possibly the best-known *Kalevala* symbol in heavy metal.

Select discography & Further reading

• **Ajattara:** *Itse* (2001). SPIKEFARM RECORDS, NAULA021.
• **Ajattara:** *Kuolema* (2003). SPIKEFARM RECORDS, NAULA040.
• **Ajattara:** *Tyhjyys* (2004). SPIKEFARM RECORDS, NAULA053.
• **Amorphis:** *The Karelian Isthmus* (1993). RELAPSE RECORDS, NB072-2.
• **Amorphis:** *Tales From The Thousand Lakes* (1994). RELAPSE RECORDS, NB097-2.
• **Amorphis:** *Elegy* (1996). SPINEFARM RECORDS, SPI35CD.
• **Ensiferum:** *Ensiferum* (2001). SPINEFARM RECORDS, SPI112CD.
• **Ensiferum:** *Iron* (2004). SPINEFARM RECORDS SPI177CD.
• **Insomnium:** *In The Halls Of Awaiting* (2002). CANDLELIGHT RECORDS, CANDLE066CD.
• **Insomnium:** *Since The Day It All Came Down* (2004). CANDLELIGHT RECORDS, CANDLE080CD.

Samuli Knuuti: *Finnish metal. Heavy but beautiful*
www.fimic.fi > Popular Music > Articles
- General introduction to Finnish metal music.

Ajattara: www.ajattara.cjb.net
Amorphis: www.amorphis.net
Ensiferum: www.ensiferum.com
Insomnium: www.insomnium.cjb.net

Writers

Anneli Asplund, FL, is a Senior Researcher at the Folklore Archives of the Finnish Literature Society.

Antti Häyrynen is a freelance music journalist in Helsinki.

Samuli Knuuti is a journalist from Espoo specializing in popular culture and literature.

Pekko Käppi is a student of ethnomusicology in Tampere and of folkloristics in Turku.

Pekka Laaksonen, FT hc, Professor, was director of the Folklore Archives of the Finnish Literature Society until 2004. He is also chairman of the Kalevala Society.

Timo Leisiö, FT, is Professor of Ethnomusicology at the Department of Music Anthropology of the University of Tampere. At the moment he is working on a unitary theory for the modal analysis of all music in the world.

Sirkka-Liisa Mettomäki, FM, is Communications Officer with the Finnish Literature Society and was secretary of the Kalevala Society from 1990 to 2000.

Matti Riekki is the editor-in-chief of *Hamara*, a magazine specializing in heavy rock, and co-host of *Metalliliitto*, a heavy metal music programme on the national YleX radio channel. He is also a freelance journalist involved in this, that and the other.

Harri Römpötti is a freelance journalist specializing in popular culture and world music.

Helena Ruhkala, FM, MuM, is Director of the Folk Music Institute and Cultural Director of the Folk Arts Centre in Kaustinen.

Petri Silas is a music journalist and music critic. His articles have been published on the pages of Finland's second biggest daily newspaper *Aamulehti*, the leading local rock magazine *Soundi* and various magazines specializing in music such as *Rytmi*, *Rondo* and *Finnish Music Quarterly*.

Hannu Tolvanen, FM in Musicology (University of Helsinki), is writing a doctoral dissertation on Finnish rock music. He has been employed at the Sibelius Academy since 1989.

Index of persons

Only contains names of persons referred to in the articles proper.